T0171430

AWARE AND PREPARED

A Guide to Personal Safety and Security for Everyone

Ronald K. Hanzel

iUniverse, Inc.
Bloomington

Aware and Prepared
A Guide to Personal Safety and Security for Everyone

Copyright © 2011 Ronald K. Hanzel

iUniverse books may be ordered through booksellers or by contacting:

iUniverse
1663 Liberty Drive
Bloomington, IN 47403
www.iuniverse.com
1-800-Authors (1-800-288-4677)

ISBN: 978-1-4502-8208-6 (pbk)
ISBN: 978-1-4502-8210-9 (ebk)

Library of Congress Control Number: 2010919510

Printed in the United States of America

iUniverse rev. date: 1/25/2011

Acknowledgments

Special thanks to my instructor and mentor in Kenpo karate, ninth-degree black belt Mr. Mark Miller. His insight and inspiration for the past thirty-seven years have given me the ability to see many different situations from many different angles. His knowledge of the history and art of Kenpo is priceless.

Thanks to Grand Master Mr. Al Tracy, with whom I had the wonderful experience of working one-on-one when I had my studio. His enthusiasm during those visits helped me stay focused. In one of the best seminars I have ever attended, he shared a wealth of information and in-depth understanding of the ancient history and origin of martial arts, as well as the "karate boom" of the late 1960s and early 1970s. I would also like to thank Mr. Tracy for letting me use the names of the techniques in chapter 7 for the self-defense portion of the book.

The pictures and video that are associated with this book would not have been possible without help from Michael Eames, third-degree black belt in Kenpo, and Ted Majewski, fifth-degree black belt in White Krane gung fu and third-degree black belt in Kenpo. Thanks, Michael, for being so patient while I executed the techniques on you for the pictures and the video. Ted was the cameraman I could not do without. Making the video and photographs was a real blast. Thanks to Christine Sekerak, student of Kenpo, who helped with key techniques in the photographs.

David Ruiz, third-degree black belt in Kenpo and a true master with the computer, helped me with editing and graphics in the video.

James Porowski, MEd, helped me with the first proof of the manuscript and corrected the grammar and spelling errors that I made finishing this book. Thanks again, James.

Thanks to my wonderful family—my wife Sandra, son Ronald and daughter Tina—for being so patient with me while I was writing this book.

Finally, I will be donating 20 percent of the net profit to the Wounded Warrior Foundation. Another 20 percent of the book's net profit will go the St. Jude Children's Research Hospital.

Disclaimer and Warning

When you need help *now*, just remember the police are only minutes away. Remember, help can come from people who see what is happening from inside their home, on the street, or in their cars. This book does not claim to have all the answers. No one has *all* the answers. Reading this book not just once but several times will enable you to become more aware of your surroundings and increase your chances of stopping a problem before it starts. Do not just read it once and let it sit on a shelf or give it to someone and forget the contents. Read this book several times. Use markers, highlighters, or Post-its to mark ideas that are important to you. Try to implement just a few ideas from this book every week, and you will be more confident and aware in a very short time. Do not try to change everything you do all at once. Count on no one but yourself to stay safe. Many things are mentioned more than once throughout this book. This was no accident. We all learn by repetition or by seeing or reading things more than once.

As I wrote this book, I received many e-mails about different types of cons and scams. Trying to keep track of all of them and verifying their validity would prevent me from ever completing this book. Therefore, it is up to you to watch for new cons and scams; pay attention to the e-mail you receive and listen to friends who may have heard of different versions. Be sure to verify and check out any and all cons and scams you may hear about. This is about the only way you can keep up with them.

In chapter 7 I cover self-defense. Should you decide to seek self-defense training, please be sure to insist on qualified, experienced instruction from a reputable school—seek someone you feel has your best interest at heart, not just your money. The self-defense techniques offered in this book give you a few ideas, out of many hundreds of ways, about countering an attack. Never forget that when you execute the moves in this book or any moves taught to you in a self-defense class, some moves may hurt *you*. However, this should be what I call "an even exchange." In other words, the damage you do to your opponent should be many times more painful and damaging to them than what you encounter executing the technique. For example, if you punch someone in the face, you may hurt your hand. You get a bruised knuckle; they get a broken nose or cut above or below the eye. You hit them with an elbow, and you may bruise your elbow (example: if you hit them in the chin with an upward elbow or sandwich their face with a horizontal forearm; see chapter 7). Their injuries are going to be far worse than anything that can happen to you.

CONTENTS

INTRODUCTION
Why This Book? Why Now?

Growing up and going to school, I always seemed to be the underdog. Try as I might, my skill level was not always where I wanted it to be. We lived in a very small neighborhood of dead-end streets, where we baby boomers would play baseball and football. I got along well with the dozen or so children in my limited area. Once outside that comfort zone, I quickly found that my ability was not what I had hoped it would be in the real world. I had always wanted to learn martial arts, believing that would help equalize my lack of size and power. At the age of twenty-one, working full-time and making a good income, I decided to finally take that step toward learning self-defense. I went to many different schools and studios to observe classes, but I didn't care for the group class environment. Then I found a school that taught private lessons. And I could try five lessons first before making any decision. The private lessons gave me the training I needed to progress at my own pace and ask questions without feeling inferior. Four years later I tested for my first-degree black belt. At the age of thirty, having obtained my second-degree black belt, I opened the third franchise for that studio. As much as I enjoyed having my own business and was proud of teaching others, working full time and operating the school full time took their toll. So with deep regret I sold the school after almost thirteen years. The love of teaching and helping others never left me. After retiring from my full-time job in 2005, I started teaching again on a part-time basis. One of the classes was at a local college. Teaching senior citizens about assault awareness and prevention gave me great satisfaction. Locally I would give seminars on that subject and provide handouts for the awareness part of the seminar. At one of the last seminars, I gave out eleven pages instead of the usual three or four pages. I thought to myself, "This is almost like giving them a book." That's when it hit me—why not a book? The more research I did, the more information I found, and everything just flowed.

Then I checked out the FBI website. There is so much information there it would take volumes of books to give you the statistics. Instead, I will provide an overview. If you need for more information, you can go online to FBI.gov and check out Crime in the United States 2007, the most current statistics as I wrote this book. You can spend hours looking at different sites and statistics. The following is a brief summary of the statistics from that site. Even though most crimes have decreased very slightly, I think it is very important to help bring them down even more. Look at the statistics and check your region on the charts below to see how your region compares to other regions.

Violent Crime

In the FBI's Uniform Crime Reporting (UCR) Program, violent crime includes four offenses: murder and non-negligent manslaughter, forcible rape, robbery, and aggravated assault. Violent crimes are defined in the UCR Program as those offenses which involve force or threat of force.

The data presented in *Crime in the United States* reflects the Hierarchy Rule, which requires that only the most serious offense in a multiple-offense criminal incident be counted. The descending order of UCR violent crimes are murder and non-negligent manslaughter, forcible rape, robbery, and aggravated assault.

- Aggravated assault accounted for 60.8 percent of violent crimes, the highest number of violent crimes reported to law enforcement. Robbery comprised 31.6 percent, and forcible rape accounted for 6.4 percent. Murder accounted for 1.2 percent of the estimated violent crimes in 2007.
- In 2007, offenders used firearms in 68.0 percent of the nation's murders, 42.8 percent of robberies, and 21.4 percent of aggravated assaults. (Weapons data are not collected for forcible rape offenses.) (based on the *Robbery Table 3, Aggravated Assault*) Nationwide, an estimated 1,408,337 violent crimes occurred in 2007.
- There were an estimated 466.9 violent crimes per 100,000 inhabitants.

When data for 2007 were compared with 2006 data, the estimated volume of violent crime declined 0.7 percent. To see the table and Expanded Homicide Data Table 6, go to the FBI website and look up Crime in the United States 2007.

Robbery Table 3
Robbery, types of weapons used, percent distribution by region, 2007.

| Region | Total all weapons[1] | Armed | | | Strong-arm |
		Firearms	Knives or cutting instruments	Other weapons	
Total	100.0	42.8	8.3	9.0	39.9
Northeast	100.0	34.6	10.5	8.3	46.6
Midwest	100.0	43.7	6.4	9.0	41.0
South	100.0	50.4	7.4	9.0	33.2
West	100.0	34.8	9.6	9.4	46.2

Note: because of rounding, percentages may not add up to 100.

Aggravated Assault Table
Aggravated Assault, types of weapons used, percent distribution by region, 2007.

Region	Total all weapons[1]	Firearms	Knives or cutting instruments	Other weapons (clubs, blunt objects, etc.)	Personal weapons (hands, fists, feet, etc.)
Total	100.0	21.4	18.8	34.2	25.7
Northeast	100.0	15.2	20.9	33.9	30.1
Midwest	100.0	22.2	17.4	31.2	29.2
South	100.0	23.4	19.5	34.5	22.6
West	100.0	19.9	17.3	35.4	27.4

Note: because of rounding, percentages may not add up to 100.

Expanded Homicide Data Table 6
Murder, types of weapons used, percent distribution by region, 2007.

Region	Total all weapons[1]	Firearms	Knives or cutting instruments	Unknown or other dangerous weapons	Personal weapons (hands, fists, feet, etc.)[2]
Total	100.0	68.0	12.1	14.1	5.8
Northeast	100.0	66.6	14.8	13.4	5.1
Midwest	100.0	66.0	10.6	17.4	5.9
South	100.0	69.7	11.3	13.8	5.2
West	100.0	67.6	13.0	12.6	6.9

Notes: because of rounding, percentages may not add up to 100; pushed is included in personal weapons.

Property Crime

In the FBI's Uniform Crime Reporting (UCR) Program, property crime includes burglary, larceny-theft, motor vehicle theft, and arson. The object of theft-type offenses is the taking of money or property, without force or threat of force against the victims. The property crime category includes arson because the offense involves the destruction of property; however, arson victims may be subjected to force. Because of limited participation and varying collection procedures by local law enforcement agencies, only limited data are available for arson. Arson statistics are included in trend, clearance, and arrest tables throughout *Crime in the United States,* but they are not included in any estimated volume data. The arson section in this report provides more information on the offense.

According to the Hierarchy Rule, which requires that only the most serious offense in a multiple-offense criminal incident be counted, in descending order of severity are the property crimes of burglary, larceny-theft, and motor vehicle theft. The Hierarchy Rule does not apply to the offense of arson.

- In the nation in 2007, there were an estimated 9,843,481 property crime offenses.
- When comparing 2007 data to that of 2006, the two-year trend showed property crime decreased 1.4 percent. The ten-year trend,

comparing 2007 with 1998, presented a 10.1 percent drop in property crime.

- The rate of property crimes was estimated at 3,263.5 offenses per 100,000 inhabitants in 2007. This represented a 2.1 percent decrease compared to the rate in 2006.
- Larceny-theft offenses accounted for over two-thirds (66.7 percent) of all property crimes in 2007.
- In 2007, an estimated 17.6 billion dollars in losses resulted from property crimes. (For property crimes there are many tables to compare on the FBI website for further data.)

Burglary
- In 2007, there were an estimated 2,179,140 burglaries, a decrease of 0.2 percent compared with 2006 data.
- An examination of 5- and 10-year trends reveals an increase of 1.1 percent in the number of burglaries when compared with the 2003 estimate and a decline of 606 percent when compared with the 1998 estimate.
- Burglary accounted for 22.1 percent of the estimated number of property crimes committed in 2007.
- Of all burglaries, 61.1 percent involved forcible entry, 32.4 percent were unlawful entries (without force), and the remainder (6.5 percent) were forcible entry attempts.
- In 2007, burglary offenses cost victims an estimated $4.3 billion in lost property; overall, the average dollar loss per burglary offense was $1,991.
- Burglary of residential properties accounted for 67.9 percent of all burglary offenses.
- Offenses for which time of occurrence was known show that 57.4 percent of burglaries took place during the day and 42.6 percent at night.
- Offenses for which time of occurrence was known showed that more residential burglaries (63.6 percent) occurred during the daytime, while 56.4 percent of nonresidential burglaries occurred during the nighttime hours.

(Detailed facts with the percentages are available on the FBI website.)

Larceny-Theft

The FBI's Uniform Crime Reporting Program defines larceny-theft as the unlawful taking, carrying, or riding away of property from the possession or constructive possession of another. Examples are thefts of bicycles, motor vehicle parts and accessories, shoplifting, pocket-picking, or the stealing of any property or article that is not taken by force and violence or by fraud. Attempted larcenies are included. Embezzlement, confidence games, forgery, check fraud, etc., are excluded. (Author's note: During my childhood several of my bicycles were stolen. However my father used metal stamping lettering in several places with my name, address, and phone number, which did recover a few bicycles.)

- During 2007, there were an estimated 6.6 million (6,568,572) larceny-thefts nationwide.
- Among all property crimes, larceny-thefts accounted for an estimated 66.7 percent in 2007.
- There was an estimated rate of 2,177.8 larceny-thefts per 100,000 inhabitants in 2007.
- When compared with the 2006 figure, there was a 0.6 percent decrease in the estimated number of larceny-thefts in 2007. When compared with the 1998 estimate, the 2007 figure showed an 11.0 percent decline.
- From 2006 to 2007, the rate of larceny-thefts declined 1.3 percent, and from 1998 to 2007, the rate declined 20.2 percent.
- Larceny-theft offenses cost victims an estimated $5.8 billion dollars in lost property in 2007.
- The average value of property taken during larceny-thefts was $886 per offense.

Expanded offense data are the details of the various offenses that the Program collects beyond the count of how many crimes law enforcement agencies report. These details may include the type of the weapons used in a crime, type or value of items stolen, and so forth. In addition, expanded data include trends (for example, two-year comparisons) and rates per 100,000 inhabitants. Expanded information regarding larceny-theft is available at the FBI site stated earlier. (Author's note: not all of the larceny-theft offenses are covered in this book).

CHAPTER ONE
Awareness on the Home Front

I may be sitting in my big, comfortable recliner with my feet up, watching the ball game or one of my favorite programs. Maybe I'm working in the front yard on the flowerbed, with my back to the street, or maybe I'm cutting the grass or working in the garden in the back yard. My mind is relaxed, without a care in the world. Never in my wildest dreams, or maybe nightmares, would I feel threatened. This is *my* house, *my* home, dare I say *my* castle.

Most of us feel this way, secure and safe—no worries while we do what needs to be done around the house. Our thoughts go to the children or grandchildren. Hey, how about that round of golf the other day when you couldn't putt to save your life? Most of us feel safe and secure when we are at home.

Today, with unemployment around 9.5 or 10 percent, far more in some states, the threat of home invasion or assault is becoming a reality that can affect everyone. There is no discrimination based on age, sex, religion, race, or even social status. We are all susceptible to crime, even though FBI statistics show a slight decrease in certain areas. As for me, I do not want to be part of the FBI statistics, and I am sure you don't either.

This book will deal with becoming more aware on the home front, and, with the economy going downhill fast, also while traveling, shopping, and investing, which become more important every day. Just because you are in your twenties or thirties, don't think you are safe from assaults or a home burglary. Many points in this book will be helpful; some seem to be simple common sense, yet most of us don't even think to apply them until it is too late.

If your home has an attached garage, keep the garage door closed when working in the house. "I live in an upscale neighborhood" or "my neighbors help keep the neighborhood safe" are famous last words from a person who has yet to have a snow blower or expensive golf clubs taken from an open garage. Or, even worse, someone enters your home and assaults you, robs you, or maybe … I don't want to even go there, but you know what I mean.

First and foremost, if you suspect that your home has been broken into upon arriving home, *do not go inside!* Go to a neighbor if necessary and call 911, or park a few houses away and call 911 from your cell phone. It is always best to be on the side of caution rather than to risk your own personal safety. A strange car parked in your driveway is a sign to be cautious. Shades or blinds that are closed when you get home that you know you left open is another "beware" signal, especially if the window or door was not open when you left the house. A window or door that may be open or broken when you get home is a not a good sign either.

When you return home or anytime you need to open the overhead garage door to get into the garage, it only takes a second to push the button to close the garage door. Try to get into the habit of closing the door when your vehicle is completely in the garage before you exit the vehicle. Many times we get so caught up in our daily lives and routines we don't think of something as simple pushing the button to close the garage door when we get home. We have a call to make or groceries to put away or maybe a dog to let outside. There are many distractions that can take our minds off something so minor, so simple. As you have seen from the introduction *Why This Book? Why Now?* (check the FBI statistics), a crime can happen to anyone, anywhere, at any time. Have we become so self-centered as to think it can't happen to us because we know better? That kind of thinking can be very costly.

While working in the front yard, stay alert if anyone approaches from the street. Don't be so focused on the flowers or painting the front porch that you become oblivious to anyone walking toward you from the street. This could be a salesman, someone asking for directions, or even a Girl Scout selling your favorite cookies.

The weather is getting nicer. It is time to plant the flowers in the front yard by the front window and porch. You gather all the gardening tools you need for the job. You are trying to decide which flowers go where and how to make your yard look like a professional landscaper spent weeks getting the yard in the shape you wanted. However, being aware of what is going on around you could save you a lot of trouble. You are working on the flowerbed, sitting on a work stool, the kind that stores all the tools you just took out of the garage next to you or under the seat. Be sure one of those "tools" is either a working cordless phone or, even better, a cell phone. Notice any vehicles that may drive past your home more than two or three times. Devious people look for easy targets and may drive up and down a street several times before they decide which place may be the easiest target.

I am often asked about pepper spray and if it really works. The answer is yes. However, there is something else that most homeowners use that is just as effective and can hit your target at a greater distance. Wasp spray usually has a range of fifteen to twenty feet, and you can direct it more accurately. Keep a can near you while working in the yard; it may be a good idea to have cans in other areas in the house as well. Just aim it at the face of any assailant; it works the same as pepper spray.

When you are working in the back yard, whether cutting the grass, working in the garden, or playing with the dog, be sure to keep the garage door closed. It only takes a few seconds for someone to pull into the driveway and take your golf clubs or expensive bicycle. If you have an attached garage, intruders may also go into your home. Bring an extra remote opener with you if you walk the dog or are in the back yard.

All household doors to the outside should have a good quality dead bolt. If there is a window near the door or a door with a window in it within reach of the dead bolt, install the kind that needs a key on both the inside and the outside of the lock. Never leave the key in the lock on the inside. Put the key where anyone in the home can reach it easily to unlock the door in case of an emergency. Hiding a spare key under a doormat or fake rocks could spell trouble. An extra one in your wallet or left with a trusted neighbor or nearby relatives may be a better idea.

Door frames should be checked to be sure the wood is solid and in good shape. Solid framing is a must if the dead bolts are going to do the job for which they are designed. There are many types of doors and locking devices from which to choose. (The author does not endorse any make or brand or doors or locks.) Speaking of locks and doors: many homes have double sliding glass doors leading to the back yard or deck. Simple devices such as a broomstick handle or piece of wood set in the track will prevent the door from opening even if left unlocked. The locks provided with sliding doors are usually of questionable quality. It doesn't take a genius, however, to figure out that if you break the window, you can remove the broomstick handle or simply climb through the opening to gain access. Alert neighbors in nearby homes may minimize this risk, but a break-in can still happen.

A good way to evaluate the security of your locks and doors is to have your local police department send someone out to your home to check your house to be sure there are no easy access points of which you are unaware. They can help you decide what type of locks, doors, or other security devices you may need. Most suburbs and small towns will provide this service. In larger cities, you may need to hire a private company to provide this service. Many alarm companies will come out and provide a free inspection in the hope of selling you an alarm. If you just want an inspection, tell them you are getting several estimates, and evaluate their suggestions. You may want to make some changes to your home security based on what they had to say. If you use a private company or companies, always check with the Better Business Bureau to find a reputable company.

Your doorbell rings while you are in the kitchen and you think, "I'm really not expecting anyone." You open the door … *wham*. Someone forces his or her way into your house. It happens every day. The intruder might look like a telephone repairman, police, or any number of other trustworthy people. Today we must take more precautions and always look before opening the door to anyone. If you did not call to have someone come to your home for any repairs, be ready to question their motives. Utility workers all carry company-issued identification with their name and picture. Check to see if the associated vehicle for that company is in your driveway or parked in the street. Also, if you have any doubt about who they are, ask them to wait and call that company to see why they are there before letting them in your home. The same can be said about police, firemen, rescue squads, and any number of public servants. Always check to be sure that they are legitimate.

If your front door does not have a peephole or window to view who is at the door, have a peephole installed. Be sure that it is at the proper height for you and anyone in your house. Keeping yourself, your home, and your possessions safe is not paranoid or old-fashioned. In the world today it is essential. It's common to hear "He/she looked so professional" or "They were so clean-cut that I never imagined …" all the time in the news. Don't let yourself become one of those victims. Those who live alone, especially women and the elderly, are more likely to become victimized by this type of criminal.

Home Lighting

Make sure all porches and entrances are well-lit. Lights on the outside of your garage, attached or detached, should be installed. The kind that detects movement is most common. The driveway leading to the garage should have a light that comes on at dusk and turns off at dawn. This is especially important if your local city or government does not provide streetlights, as in many rural areas. If your garage or house is set back from the street a distance so the street lighting is not sufficient, you may need one or more lights along the driveway. Back yards should also have motion detector lights. Whether a deer, dog, cat, or person is roaming around in your back yard, you'll want to light it up to view what is outside.

Inside your home, when you go away, use timers for lamps, radios, and even the television if you don't expect to be home until well after dark. It might be a good idea to have lamps in different parts of the house plugged into timers that turn on and off at staggered times throughout the evening. This gives the illusion someone is home. If you will be gone more than a couple of days, consider having a timer for a radio during the day and another for the television in the evening.

Get to know your neighbors. If you are new to a neighborhood, start by introducing yourself to the neighbors on both sides of your home. Being able to trust new neighbors, for some, can take a long time. You need to trust your gut feelings, in many cases. First impressions are very important. If you get a bad vibe, don't shut that person out; give it some time and see if how you feel changes. Sometimes it may take several months to become comfortable about trusting people. Meeting the parents of your children's playmates is important on two fronts. First and foremost, you need to know that your child is safe if he or she spends any time at their home. There are many websites where you can check names and address to see if you have anything to worry about. Too cautious, maybe. Too paranoid, possibly. However, it's better to be cautious than to end up saying, "If I had only known." Also, this is just another way to learn to trust your neighbors. If you live on a main street or busy side street, you can't be too cautious, and you need to have people you trust nearby.

Any time you arrive at home, whether or not you decide to go into the garage, be sure you are not being followed. Usually it is a good idea to start looking in the rearview mirror a couple of blocks from home. If you think you are being followed, drive around the block. Another way to check if you are being followed is to pull into a neighboring driveway to turn around and then head back in the direction from which you came. I am addressing this issue in this section because if you have an attached garage, this safety check can be your first line of defense in securing your safety and your home. All too often we don't pay enough attention to who or what is behind us when we arrive at home. Should you believe you are being followed, call 911 on your cell phone. If you do not have a cell phone with you, drive to the nearest police station or fire station.

Try not to be a creature of habit. If you own a dog and walk it daily, try not to take the same route. Vary the times when you walk. If you walk or jog for exercise, the same can be said about those times and routes. When going to work, leave at different times and try different routes to get there, but be familiar with any and all routes you take. You don't want to try going to work on roads you are unfamiliar with, as you could wind up in an undesirable neighborhood. If driving a new route, find out if there are any detours. This can save you time and headaches. Portable GPS navigators are a great way to travel to destinations you have not been to before. But they can take you through areas that could be unsafe for most travelers. If you are in a city you are familiar with, check with someone who knows the route you are going to take, and be sure you won't go through a high-crime area. When shopping at the mall or even just for groceries, don't be a "creature of habit" and shop at the same time and day every week. When we become creatures of habit, we become complacent and an easy target.

You get a phone call at work; the cousin whom you grew up with but haven't seen in five years just got in town. You tell him or her the key is in a fake rock next to the front steps. That's never been a problem before. However, someone driving past your home saw your cousin and where the key was hidden. Three weeks later, your jewelry, big screen television, and lock box with the "extra" cash you keep for emergencies are missing when you get home from work. There's no sign of forced entry, but the rock where you hid the key is overturned.

Being sensible about all the keys you have is another very important part of home security. Hiding keys under the doormat or flowerpot, for example, is not very wise. If you have your address tag on your key ring, remove it as soon as possible. A number of people get up every morning trying to figure out how to take what does not belong to them from the rest of us. You lose your keys, and someone arrives at your house with them in hand. You thank them and maybe even give them a small reward. You feel like there are some decent people in the world. How do you know they didn't make copies of those keys? Whether keys are for your home, car, or where you work, you can't be too cautious. Change the locks for whichever keys were returned. If some keys were for work, be sure to notify them in writing, to protect yourself in case any problems arise.

It is far better to have two extra copies of every key than to have your address or phone number on them in case you lose them. Keep one spare set hidden at home and the other in a safe deposit box. If you don't have a safe deposit box, get one. They are not expensive and the fee is tax deductible. Sometimes older children, relatives, or even a trusted neighbor should have an extra house key. However, only *you* know whom you can trust and how much you can trust them. I keep an extra house key in my wallet. I'm in my midfifties and I have never lost a wallet, so I feel comfortable to have it there. It may not be such a good idea for women to put extra keys in a wallet that is in their purse.

Harassing or Obscene Phone Calls

This type of problem is not as common as it was fifteen or twenty years ago. If you have a landline (not cellular), most of the phone service providers offer custom calling features. Three of them you should become familiar with are *57, *69, and caller ID. The *57 feature traces the call. The information will then be on record at the phone company and available for the local police. The *69 feature is an automatic callback feature that will dial the last caller. Caller ID displays the phone number of the phone calling you, unless it is a non-published or unlisted private number. You can call your local phone company's business office and ask for the number of the Annoyance Call Bureau. You can also visit their website for information about bomb threats, collect calls, obscene calls, and various other types of annoying calls.

A few tips: Keep a log of annoying calls, including date, time, what was said or what happened during the call, and how long the call lasted. Do not slam the handset down. If the caller is threatening or making obscene comments to you, remain calm and end the conversation by saying good-bye and hanging up. Try to stay calm. Many times such callers are seeking a reaction from you for their own gratification. If you get angry or slam the phone down as you hang up, that means they have succeeded and may call again at a later date. If the caller leaves a message on an answering machine, retain the message, as this may be used as evidence if needed. Keep a small recorder near the phone if calls are persistent. Notify the police and phone company if you feel threatened and give them all the information you have at that time. Keep them updated if the calls persist. As a last resort, you can have your number changed.

On a related item, never give out information over the phone indicating you are alone. Also never tell someone on the phone you will not be home at a certain time or on a certain day. If you live alone and you get a call asking to speak to your spouse, just tell them they are in the basement or busy in the garage. Then ask for a name and number to call them back. If they hang up without giving that information, pay a little more attention around the neighborhood.

CHAPTER TWO
Protecting Valuables and Other Items in Your Home

You may not have a round-the-clock guard in your apartment or home, but you can take steps to keep it safer. Part of this chapter will deal with home safety when you are not home. In the United States, there is a home burglary every fifteen seconds. Here are some tips to keep your home safer while you're away.

To start with, do not leave notes on the door when you are going on vacation or will be away for any length of time. Anyone who may come to your home for any reason will see the note and could return at a later time to help themselves to your valuables. If you live alone and work nights, do not put up a note that says do not disturb, night shift worker. This is just an invitation to anyone who learns you won't be home when it is dark, and we all know that thieves like darkness. Are your doors and windows visible from the street? Hedges and plants around the windows should be kept trimmed and not so tall as to hide the windows. With daytime break-ins on the increase, this will help reduce them. Remember, thieves always look for an easy target; they are not looking to get caught. Be sure that shrubs do not hide walkways to the front door. Some of the tips in chapter 1 can be used whether or not you are at home, such as dead bolts, sliding door locks (a stick in the door track), and many other ideas. Keeping outside lights in good working order is very important, especially motion lights. In the back yard, motion sensitive spotlights are a good idea. Depending on how wide and deep the yard is, you may need more than one. If you have several spotlights, position them to light up as much of the yard as possible.

If strangers show up at your door, do not open it. Find out what they want or need. If they want to use your phone, offer to make the call for them. To repeat, do not open the door or let them inside your home, especially if you live alone. The elderly should not let anyone they do not know inside, even if both of you are home.

Do not hesitate to report a crime or any suspicious activities. Joining a neighborhood watch group is a great idea for everyone. If your neighborhood does not have one, talk with your neighbors and get one started. This is a wise idea for single women and the elderly. There are websites that will give you an idea where convicted criminals live when you input your address, including those convicted for breaking and entering, writing bad checks, sexual offenses, and much, much more. All you need to do is type "websites for where convicted criminals live" into the search engine. At the time of this writing, 1,090,000 different sites came up. Type in the street, city, state, and zip code, and the appropriate map will show up on the screen. The site the author visited offered different colored boxes. Clicking on the box gave an address, picture, conviction, alias, description, and map for the offender. You may be surprised by how many live near you.

Walk into your home from any entrance door, front, side or back, and think like a thief. Take your time. What do you see? Money on the nightstand? Jewelry on the dresser? Don't make it easy for thieves once they enter your home. See if a wall safe or a good floor safe that can be attached to the floor with bolts is feasible. You know your home better than anyone. Try to be creative when hiding heirlooms or jewelry. Don't keep large amounts of money around the house, whether under your mattress or in a safe. Keep guns where they can be accessed if you need them but won't be easy for a stranger to find. Consult the National Rifle Association (NRA) for more information about home gun safety and gun safety with children in the home. If you have a safe deposit box, use it for things like birth certificates and other important documents. The use of portable fireproof safes for important documents is not a good idea, as they can be easily taken from your home and opened elsewhere.

If you can afford one, have a security system with monitoring stations installed. There are many companies that install and monitor security systems, and the author is not endorsing any specific company. It is a good idea to install window and door switches, as well as a motion detector. Shop around and find a company with which you feel comfortable. By shopping around and getting estimates, you also discover different ideas for protecting your home and valuables. Once you have made up your mind, it is a good idea to get references and check with the Better Business Bureau. If you cannot afford a security system, there is a less expensive alarm to signal neighbors. If your vehicle has an alarm system that will blow the horn or some kind of siren, check and see if it will work from your bedroom. If so, put the remote for you keys on your nightstand when you go to bed. Then, by pushing the panic button on the remote, your horn or any other loud signal will keep going until you turn it off or the vehicle's battery goes dead. This should scare the intruder away and alert the neighbors. Even if you park in the garage, this alarm should be effective if the homes are not too far apart. It may be helpful to share this idea with everyone you know.

Aside from being a great companion, a dog is a good security alarm. Most thieves do not want to hassle with a barking or biting dog. Large dogs are best. No matter what size dog you have, be sure to get a few beware of dog signs. Any dog will be effective if it makes enough noise so the neighbors can hear it if needed. Placing a large water and food bowl by the side or back door can also be a good idea. Some alarms even have barking and growling dog sounds—not a bad idea either.

If you are like me and pay your property taxes and insurances with one payment when due, then a safe deposit is a necessity. If the money is in my checking account or around the house, I will spend it. If I don't, my wife will certainly find a way to spend every dollar. Every month I put enough money in the safe deposit box to cover those expenses when they are due.

Most of the time thieves prefer to get in and get out quickly. If they have a difficult time finding valuables, they may leave empty-handed. Having to file only a police report and not an insurance claim is always a good thing. As I said in chapter 1, you can call your local police station and have a trained police officer assess the security of your home.

Keeping a record of your valuables is also important. Take pictures of antiques, jewelry, and television or sound systems. Your jewelry should be appraised every three to five years, based on the current price of gold, diamonds, and other precious metals and gems. If there is a spike in gold, for example, and you feel the appraisal should be updated, by all means take jewelry to a reputable jeweler, along with the most recent appraisal. A record of the make, model, and serial number of items like cameras, DVD or VCR players, camcorders, and the like should also be kept in a safe place. You can also check with your insurance agent for a rider on your home or apartment policy for any items that may need extra coverage. Expensive camera equipment with extra lenses, lighting, and accessories is an example. Another example is if you inherited jewelry from a relative that may exceed your normal policy limits.

Do not have checks mailed to your home. If at all possible, have all checks sent via direct deposit to a bank account. This includes tax refunds, social security payments, pensions, and other payments. Information is provided by the Electronic Payments Association (NACHA) at www.electronicpayments.org.

What is Direct Deposit?[1]

Direct Deposit is an electronic payment deposited directly to your checking or savings account.

How many people use Direct Deposit?

Three out of four working Americans who have Direct Deposit available for their pay use it. Ninety-seven percent of Direct Deposit users are very satisfied with it.

Do I have to use a certain financial institution to participate in Direct Deposit?

No. You may use any financial institution in the United States that is a member of the ACH Network. A very small number of financial institutions are not ACH Network members, so be sure to check with the financial institution of your choice to make sure it can accept your Direct Deposit.

Do I need to have a checking account to use Direct Deposit?

No. Your money can be deposited into any account you specify, or be distributed among different accounts.

Can I divide my pay among different accounts if I use Direct Deposit?

With Direct Deposit, you may have the option of splitting the deposit. Check with your employer or the company issuing your payment for more information.

---

1   Information from electronicpayments.org © 2009 NACHA

When can I withdraw money from payments deposited to my account using Direct Deposit?

Your money is generally available to you when your financial institution opens for business on payday.

What if my pay date falls on a holiday?

If your pay date falls on a holiday or other dates when financial institutions are closed, your money will be available on the day before your scheduled pay date.

How will I know when my payment has been deposited using Direct Deposit? How much money in taxes and deductions is withheld from my pay?

Most companies issue a dated payment stub that is identical to what you receive with a paper check. This stub shows how much was deposited into your account, the date of the deposit, and an itemized list of tax, insurance, and other deductions.

I don't want the joint owner of my checking account to know how much money I make. How can I participate in Direct Deposit?

The best way to keep transactions confidential from a joint account holder is to open another single account. Depending on the company's policy, you may be able to split your deposits among multiple accounts. Check with your employer or the company issuing your payment for more information.

What should I do if I change financial institutions?

You will need to provide your new account information to your employer or the company issuing your payment. You may also need to complete a new authorization form. Be sure to leave the old account open until the first Direct Deposit transaction appears in your new account.

What if I want to cancel my Direct Deposit?

You will need to contact the company that is sending you the Direct Deposit.

How do I sign up for Direct Deposit?

If your company offers Direct Deposit, you will be provided with an authorization form.

What if my company does not offer Direct Deposit? How can I let my employer know that I want it?

Tell your employer that you're interested in being offered Direct Deposit as a benefit. You may want to download the one-page fact sheet to show your employer the benefits of Direct Deposit.

Can my employer require me to use Direct Deposit for payroll?

Some states allow companies to mandate Direct Deposit of payroll. Contact your state for more information.

Why did my employer ask for a voided check when I signed up for Direct Deposit?

The company uses the financial institution identification number (also known as a routing transit number) as well as the account number that appear on checks to set up the Direct Deposit. The voided check is a way to make sure the information is correct.

Does Direct Deposit cost me any money?

No. Direct Deposit should not cost you anything. In fact, many financial institutions offer free checking to consumers using Direct Deposit.

With Direct Deposit, won't more people have access to my personal account information? Will my employer be able to take money out of my account?

No. Once you sign up for Direct Deposit, the information you provide simply becomes part of the transaction information read by computers. No one knows that information, and no one can withdraw money from your account.

What happens if my payment goes into someone else's account?

That's very unlikely. Should an error occur, however, simply notify the company that sent the payment.

What should I do if I have a problem with Direct Deposit?

Problems with Direct Deposit are rare because payments are made electronically. If you do have a problem, you will need to contact your employer or the company that sent you the Direct Deposit. The problem can usually be corrected immediately.

How will I be able to keep track of the balance in my account?

You will be able to manage your balances with your account statements, automated phone systems, or online.

The amount of money I receive is confidential. With Direct Deposit, can I be sure my privacy is protected?

Yes. In fact, your privacy will increase when you use Direct Deposit. Once you have authorized the Direct Deposit, computers—not people—are processing the payments. Multiple levels of security are in place to protect the payment as it passes electronically through the banking system.

What if my deposit isn't in my account on the pay date?

In the unlikely event that your deposit fails to post to your account on the scheduled pay date, contact the company that sent the payment immediately.

CHAPTER THREE
Get Rich Quick, Home Repair and Improvement Schemes, and Other Cons

Be wary of get-rich-quick opportunities or anything that requires you to pay money up front. The elderly or widows and widowers seem to be prime targets for these types of cons. The following is from an Internet site called Internet-Based Moms.[2] The author feels that this information would be helpful:

> If you're trying to earn money online, you may be tempted by opportunities that promise quick payouts and huge returns. Like most things in life, things don't usually happen that easy. If you see opportunities like this, they may use unethical methods of making money … or worse yet, be completely illegal. In many of these schemes, only a few people make money and everyone else loses their entire investment. Getting involved in these schemes is never a long-term plan for financial success online.

Read the following articles to educate yourself about get-rich-quick schemes, so you'll know what to look for and avoid while working online:

- *How to Spot a Get-Rich-Quick Scheme.* There is one simple rule to spotting such scams, whether they are sales-oriented or investment-oriented. The proposal seems too good to be real. Believe your instincts, because they are right.

---

2   From the Internet site Internet-Based Moms, copyright 2002–2008

- *What Is a Pyramid Scheme?* Pyramid schemes first appeared in the latter half of the twentieth century, starting with chain letters. Basically, a pyramid scheme involves selling the possibility of earning money and does not usually involve any tangible goods.

For example, the pitch may be for "the secret to earning ten thousand dollars a month." In order to obtain that secret, you must send X dollars to the seller. What you get is nothing more than the original information or a "license" to begin selling the same "information" yourself. Ads for this type of scheme were often seen in newspapers and other mass media. The point was to sell as many opportunities as possible, before so many people were in the pyramid that the entire scheme would collapse. It got the name *pyramid scheme* because it starts with one person or a small group and expands multiple times at each level, descending from the "top," increasing the number of people involved and thus the size of the sales staff at each level. In some schemes, besides the original purchase of a secret, you were also required to send a certain fee per sale back to the person who sold you the idea. The typical features of a pyramid scheme are high-pressure sales pitches, little or no information offered about the opportunity or company prior to payment of a fee, and no contact information. If you suspect someone is operating a pyramid scheme, report it to your local sheriff's office. Remember that a pyramid scheme is not the same as multi-level marketing (MLM), where people sell things such as make-up at home parties but also earn "commissions" for enrolling new sales staff.

- *Chain Letter Pyramid Scheme.* Probably the oldest, and most familiar, pyramid scheme is the chain mail or chain letter. This is seldom seen today, mostly because there are cheaper ways to bilk people than using the US mail, and it's also illegal.

The first schemes were pitched in terms of receiving an impossible sum, like thousands of dollars, all from sending X dollars to the first person on the list included with the letter. You would then remove that person's name, add yours to the bottom, and send out ten (or more) copies to people who also wanted to become rich. Naturally, not everyone who got one of these letters participated. But the success rate was big enough to make it worth the effort, because the more letters sent out, the bigger the returns, even if your success rate was only 2 or 3 percent. Depending on how long the chain had been going, there could be several hundred or thousands of letters out there with the same list of names you got, and the first person on that list was going to make out like a bandit. As a money-making scheme, it's pretty much a dinosaur these days. Chain mail and letters do still make the rounds occasionally, usually among friends, but for the purpose of sharing things like recipes or gathering squares of material to make pillows.

- *What is a Ponzi Scheme?* The Ponzi scheme is often mistaken for, or confused with, a pyramid scheme, and while they have the same structure, they don't operate the same way.

A pyramid scheme is based on selling something intangible, like an idea, a secret to making money, or other nonexistent programs. One person sells their idea to six people for a fixed fee. Those people are then free to sell to as many people as they want, charging their own fee. The "pyramid" expands until there is virtually no market left, and the structure collapses. A Ponzi scheme typically involves investments or financial transactions of some sort. The name originated with Charles Ponzi, who emigrated to the United States from Italy in 1903. Once here, he began running the schemes to fellow immigrants who had little knowledge of the country or the language and were easily taken in. For example, the pitch may involve an investment with very complicated explanations and terms, but the bottom line is that you are promised you will earn 25 percent back in sixty days. The more you invest, the more you earn. A pitch has to be relatively slick today, containing lots of information, even if it's false, and demonstrations as to how the investment will be returned, grow with time, etc. In pyramid schemes you don't receive that type of information up front. What actually happens is something like this: Ten investors each sink $5,000 in the plan. Meanwhile, the salesman is recruiting new investors and getting their money as well. In sixty days, the person who runs the Ponzi pays those first ten investors $1,250 plus their original investment. But he didn't actually earn that money on anything. It was taken from the new group of investors and passed back along the line. The profits are made by the first levels of investors, who see their money increasing and leave it in the "kitty," getting back 25 percent in sixty days, and so on. Eventually they find out there was no kitty. Ponzis usually fall apart when someone blows the whistle, or the originator takes off with all the money, or investments have slowed to the point where returns aren't paid to the upper-level investors.

- *What Is an Illegal Matrix?* An illegal matrix is just that … illegal. It is a variation on the gifting program, where you put in X amount of dollars and your money comes from others recruited down the line. They are illegal in most states and may violate federal laws as well, because you are not providing anything tangible for the person's investment. For example, let's say you are invited to join a ladder club. You must buy a spot on the lower rung of five ladders that have a total of five rungs. That will cost you $50 for each ladder. The money paid for each ladder is distributed like this: $5 will go to each person on rungs two through five. The person at the top of the ladder gets $15, as does the ladder manufacturer (the person who started the scheme). When you recruit people, you are selling them a ladder with your name on the bottom rung. You will earn $5 from each of these people. As the levels grow, you will move up the rungs and eventually be at the top of your five ladders; you'll collect money as long as those below you continue to recruit others. But as in all pyramid style schemes, they usually collapse when someone tips off the police or the new recruits become wise to the game.

- *What Is a Gifting Program?* Gifting programs are simply a new variation on the old pyramid scheme, usually pitched as a way to share wealth or other philanthropic aims, with, of course, financial benefits to you.

The originator is level A and will recruit four people to join. They are level B. The four at level B then each go out and recruit four people of their own, who become level C. Their "gift" is $1,000. That money is passed up the levels to A. Those on level C (now sixteen people) each go out and recruit four people, who become level D. Their gift of money is passed up to the B level. Meanwhile, B is still recruiting more people for level C, whose gifts come to level A. Think of it this way: It is your "grandchildren" who make the money for you. Your vested interest is in motivating your "children" to recruit more gifters, or grandchildren, because that is how you build up funds. But as each level grows, so the market for gifters shrinks. Like all pyramid schemes, sooner or later the whole thing will collapse, because the money accrued from gifts peters out as people become aware they are not getting their funds back, and the ripple effect passes up the pyramid. These schemes are illegal in most states, and claims by programs that their "gifts" as such are tax deductions are not true.

- *What Is an HYIP?* HYIP means High-Yield Investment Program. The legitimate ones are usually investing your money in such things as commodities, FOREX, offshore, and other programs that can return up to 3 percent daily or a steady but small income over longer periods, such as a month.

As a rule of thumb, the higher the yield promised and the shorter the return period, the more likely it is that you have found a scam. While these programs are HY (high yield), they are also HR (high risk). Because the potential for earnings is so attractive, people often sink more than is required in the venture, and they can end up losing everything, even in legitimate programs. This is one way scams hook people on the idea that you can basically get rich quick. Never respond to an e-mail invitation to an HYIP. No reputable firm will advertise that way. If not a scam, it may be an e-mail harvester that logs your address into its database for selling to others. If you are intrigued by the idea of HYIP, do your homework on the company you're interested in. Never be pressured by a sales pitch that says their opportunity expires in two hours. Take some time to gather all the information you can, including what your money will be invested in; the full name, address, and location of the company you are dealing with; how you can contact them, etc. Then check with the Better Business Bureau in that city or town and see if there are any complaints against them. The more they hide, the less they really have to show you.

- *What Is an Auto-Surfer Ponzi Scheme?* A regular Ponzi scheme is one in which people are asked to invest money for what seem impossible high returns in a specified period. It is a type of pyramid scheme, with the initial levels making the most money, because the subsequent levels who are recruited invest the money paid back to people at impossible rates like 20 percent in thirty days. The same "principles" apply to the auto-surfing Ponzi scams.

Auto-surfing is a program that uses your browser to automatically surf a given number or list of sites, creating what are called page impressions, a presence on the site for X number of seconds, which is enough for that advertiser to be billed for a "hit."

There are non-Ponzi auto-surfing programs, easily recognized by the fact that they don't offer huge returns. These are run by companies who sell "hits," or page impressions, to advertisers. Typically, they will guarantee an advertiser a thousand hits for between twenty cents to a dollar. Your computer is on twenty-four hours a day, and it takes a considerable amount of time to make any money at the going rate.

Auto-surfing Ponzi schemes require an investment, for which they will guarantee you some astronomical figure like a 1 percent return every day. Let's say you invest $1,000 for that 1 percent daily return. That amounts to

$10. Your auto-surfer program would, in the honest world, have to hit 50,000 sites at a rate of .20 per thousand. But you have been given an assigned list of sites, and there are only 200 on it. To make $1 a day, they'd be paying you a rate of $50 per thousand.

What they are really doing is taking an investment paid by people you recruit and using a portion of it to pay your daily commission. Like all pyramid schemes, sooner or later they collapse when recruitment drops below the number required to keep up their payments to those above the last level.

- *What Are Paid-For Opportunities?* "Paid for" is exactly that. It is work of some kind that you are paid for. In this age of the computer, much of it relates to online business and traffic, or web page hits.

One opportunity is the "click" program. A company will assign you a list of sites, and you will be required to "land" on that page for a minimum of X seconds, usually twenty, before leaving and going on to the next. You will only be allowed to visit the site once each day and may only be required to visit all sites once, before you get a new list. Payment is either in credits per click, which accrue and are converted to cash, or in cash. However, the pay is minimal, and it takes a lot of mouse work to make a few dollars. That's why many people have gone to the auto-surfer programs. This software will open a list of sites in your browser window, moving on to the next according to a built-in timer. No hands-on work is required, but again, the pay is very minimal. Auto-surfer programs are also prone to auto-surfer Ponzi programs. Avoid these at all costs. Another opportunity is pay for clicking banners or e-mails. This works the same way as surfing sites, with credits or cash for each click. In the case of e-mails, those are usually a daily or weekly letter sent out by a company that contain paid advertising, and you are required to click through to each site. You can also earn cash by signing up for free programs from a list you are given by the company you work for. After sending them your welcome e-mail from the signup, you are credited for that site.

Although these programs may not be illegal, they are certainly unethical. When businesses pay money to advertise, they expect that potential consumers will view their ads, not people who are paid to view their ads.

- *What is a Payment Randomizer?* This is the latest in "earn money on the Internet" schemes, in which you do nothing but sit back and collect the money. Nothing is sold, and it is not a pyramid scheme. What you are banking on is other people's curiosity and desire to also earn money the way you are. Payment randomizer programs generate cash for you, just by someone opening a site in their browsers. Let's say the site is called makemoneyrandozmizer. com. The site will explain the basics of how it works, although you don't get the financial details of how much it will cost you to upgrade for a better chance to earn more money. There is a button on the page for you to join the program. If you join, you will pay a small base fee, typically $5 to $10, to the member's name that appears above the button when you click. All members' names in the program are generated randomly by the site's software. Everyone's name will appear at least once in a rotation. So if there are a thousand people in the program and the site is visited a thousand times, your name will appear at least once. Now for the "buts." Because the page is opened when your name is on it does not guarantee that the person will join. Your chance is lost for that rotation. That could happen over and over. To hedge their bets, people "upgrade" or have their name placed another X times in the rotation for an unspecified fee. When you join the program there are no guarantees of income, and you will also pay a small administration fee of $2 to $5 to the "administrator" of the site to join. It's just basically money moving around without any product—and it is quite illegal when run in this fashion.

There are many things to watch out for, such as work-at-home schemes, door-to-door sales, telephone sales, supplemental health insurance, miracle cures, bargain prices for glasses or hearing aids from unknown sources, and unfamiliar charities.

Another type of scheme or con would be to invest in real estate that you have not seen or can't get to because of distance; i.e., in a different state. But you are shown a picture of what you would be buying. If these were such good deals and you found them, would you share with strangers? No matter if it is a home or property for sale, when you are investing in real estate or property, know your source, get an attorney, and never invest money you can't afford to lose. Dealing with a reputable mortgage company is also very important. Anytime you make any real estate purchase, have your attorney look over the papers. It's a small price for peace of mind. Do not overextend yourself with payments. Have the home inspected by a reputable contractor. *Don't trust the real estate agent to select the inspector.* You can also check with the Better Business Bureau to see if there have been any complaints. Watch out for someone who promises a very high rate of return on your investment with little or no risk on your part.

The following is information on how to avoid real estate scams by Grace Bloodwell on the website HowToDoThings.com.[3]

If you are in the market to buy or sell a house or refinance your mortgage, or if you are considering investing in the real estate world, beware—there are scams out there that the smartest people fall for. Here some of the classic real estate scams and tips on how to avoid them.

Who is the Ideal Con Artist? The savviest of con artists are those who have already attained some level of trust in your life. People you deal with daily, even family members, prove the most successful of con artists. When we "go along with others," our brains' defense mechanisms soften, and our skepticism is reduced. Con artists use this neurological trick to get you. It is okay to place trust in your friends, family, and co-workers, but be skeptical about any business pitches they may give you. Always seek the advice of two or more financial advisors or confidants before proceeding.

Overseas Investment and Return. Con artists who utilize this real estate scam play on a victim's deepest desire: getting something for little—an easy investment. These schemes are usually Ponzi schemes, meaning con artists collect money from many victims and disperse smaller amounts out to the same people from the same pool of money and claim it is "profit." In this model, investors are told to send investment checks, and they are given small checks in return, supposedly "proving" the system works. In reality they are receiving a small chunk of change from another "investor" who has also fallen for this plot. People tend to fall for the overseas angle because it is exotic-sounding, and they think they are, in some way, taking advantage of a new discovery or resource others are not aware of.

> *Defense:* Ask yourself the simple question, "Is this too good to be true?" Examine the business model thoroughly to determine whether the model could actually work. If you have never invested in real estate before, it is a good idea to start local, not abroad.

Local Investment Scam. People are caught more off-guard when con artists use familiar landmarks or names. For instance, if someone calls you out of the blue to invest in a building across the world, it may raise your eyebrows. However, if the building is the very building you pass by on your morning

3   Grace Bloodwell, "How To Avoid Real Estate Scams," HowToDoThings.com

commute, it may be more believable. Similar to investing in overseas real estate, you should be wary of anything that sounds too good to be true.

Defense: Always investigate beyond the surface. Go to the site. Ask your contact person for a letter of credentials and show the document to officials at the building site. If they have never heard of this investment company, chances are you were almost duped.

Internet Advance Fee Fraud. In this real estate scam the individuals doing the trickery will ask for a down payment in order to get you your return. They will ask you to wire a small amount of money to "free" up channels that will ultimately return profits from a commercial or residential project. These scam artists simply collect a few dollars from hundreds and thousands of people—giving them a hefty and easy profit.

Defense: Never wire money over the Internet.

Title Fraud. In this scheme the con artist steals a home owner's identity and is thus able to take title of the home. In some cases, mortgages have been drawn against properties without the knowledge of the actual homeowner.

Defense: Visit <u>Protect Your Title</u>, where you can find tips on guarding your privacy and home. Always be cautious against giving your social security number out, as well as other private information.

Home Equity Stripping. Home equity stripping occurs when a lender says it's okay to exaggerate your personal wealth. They approve you for an amount you cannot afford and then strip you of it. They can take your home and more for nonpayment.

Defense: Do not continue with the loan if the lender implies that you can embellish on your application.

Home Equity Flipping. This when a lender encourages you to repeatedly refinance your loans at what they say are better rates each time, only to nail you with additional fees and interest for each new loan. This scam takes a longer time to show itself and can be hard to detect since the lender leads you to believe that each loan refinance is the smartest and least expensive move. Since the interest and debt will keep adding up, eventually this scam can result in you losing your home.

Defense: Make sure you know what the rates and fees are when you refinance.

Home Improvement Scam. A typical scam with contractors is when they tell the homeowner that they can find a lender who will help them finance a project when the homeowner cannot afford it on their own. The contractor and a lender he knows offer a financing plan and make the homeowner quickly sign papers. In reality these papers are for a home equity loan with high rates—rates that you are now required to pay off. The contractor will most likely do a poor job on the project, and you may be stuck with high payments on a poorly constructed home.

Defense: Work only with contractors you trust and who have good reputations.

All of the above are typical real estate scams, but this list is not all-inclusive.

Always remember that while it's true that any investment is a risk, taking risks does not always translate into profit. Always examine the underlying business model your contact is presenting and ask yourself (and other people you trust) if it makes sense. If you think it is too good to be true, it probably is.

Another common type of scam aimed primarily at the elderly and uninformed is that they owe money for a debt from a deceased relative.

A relative passes away or is hospitalized. You get a phone call or registered letter, or someone comes to the front door, stating the relative owed money for some item or service. You may not have any idea if this is true or not, but because they give names, your relationship and other pertinent information, it sounds possible. Don't buy their claims. Unless you are the guardian, co-signer, or some other type of trustee, you owe nothing. This is a big scam that has been around for a long time. Get the information and tell them you will get back to them; meanwhile, contact other relatives or the authorities.

Scammers may ask you to send your social security number because you were left a large amount of money. Ask for proof before you give them anything. Get the name of the company for which they work. Ask how they found you. Do some research on their company. If you run into a problem and need more information, get an attorney. I know I have said that a couple of times already. Personally I don't like attorneys, but when you need one, they are great to have around.

Watch out for bargains on home repairs or improvements, especially after severe weather, such as a thunderstorm, tornado, or snowstorm. Single female homeowners, the elderly, and widows and widowers seem to be targeted more often.

Beware of unlicensed contractors!

If you are planning a home improvement project, like a deck, a new bathroom, or a garage, you will probably need to hire a building contractor.[4]

Not an easy task …

There is no shortage of building contractor horror stories. Almost everyone has heard tales of damage, scams, shoddy workmanship, and builders who disappear in the middle of a project. In fact, except for auto repair shops and car dealerships, no other industry has generated as many complaints, according to the Council of Better Business Bureaus. It would seem that finding a reliable and qualified contractor is not an easy task.

You can put the odds on your side, however, by making sure you hire only licensed contractors.

Hazards of hiring the unlicensed
While licensing isn't necessarily a measure of competence, it does imply a certain level of professionalism and suggests that the contractor is committed to his or her job. More significantly, licensing can protect you from a number of potential problems, such as the following:

- **Unlicensed usually means uninsured**. If you use a contractor who is uninsured, it means the contractor has no way of reimbursing you for any property damage he or she causes. This means you end up paying the price. Likewise, if contractor carelessness leads to injury or damage to someone else's property, the problem is likely to become yours.
- **No coverage under homeowner's policy.** Some homeowners believe it is safe to use an uninsured contractor, assuming that any damages incurred would be covered under their *own* insurance policies. However, this isn't the case. Most homeowner policies require that licensed contractors do any work to the property; coverage is often specifically excluded for damages caused by "bootleg" contractors.
- **Noncompliance with building codes.** Most building projects, even minor ones, usually require permits and inspections. Unlicensed contractors are often unfamiliar with the applicable building codes and are unable to obtain permits. If your project

4   http://www.eastlongmeadow.org/Building/beware.htm

26

isn't permitted or doesn't comply with building and zoning codes, you may—and probably will—be ordered to remove or repair the job. Even if a building inspector doesn't "catch" your code violation right away, you will almost certainly have to correct it if and when you try to sell your house.

- **Poor quality work**. Not all unlicensed contractors do poor quality work. And not all poor quality work is done by unlicensed contractors. However, as a rule, if there's shoddy work to be done, it's usually done by unlicensed contractors. Because unlicensed contractors aren't subject to meeting specific standards, they are often untrained, less experienced, and unqualified to do certain types of work.

Sloppy work by an unlicensed contractor could have serious ramifications. "Basically, it's a safety hazard if your work isn't done properly," says Brett Martin, Communications Manager for the National Association of the Remodeling Industry. "If it's not structurally sound, if it's not wired properly, obviously you could face major consequences at some point."

- **Con artists**. Scams in the construction industry, especially in the home improvement business, have become almost legendary in the last few decades. Con artists posing as qualified contractors, often targeting the elderly, have made national news any number of times. Even so, unwary homeowners continue to be taken in by these pseudo contractors, who often promise unrealistically low prices or use scare tactics to close the deal. In those cases, the homeowner typically ends up with either an incomplete or a low quality improvement project—and several hundred, or even thousands, of dollars less.
- **Limited recourse for broken contracts**. If you have a dispute with a licensed contractor, you can call his or her licensing agency. Some licensing agencies offer mediation services or maintain a guaranty fund to help consumers recover their losses. At the very least, the licensing agency has the authority to suspend or revoke a dishonest contractor's license. While this doesn't necessarily ensure a contractor will play fair, it gives him or her considerably more incentive to do so. Regulatory authorities, however, cannot take this sort of action against unlicensed contractors. Therefore, homeowners often find that their only recourse is a civil lawsuit. And because many unlicensed contractors go in and out of business readily, such a lawsuit is frequently a waste of time.

Consumers in some states do not even have this option. In areas where licensing is required, contracts with unlicensed contractors may be legally unenforceable.

Warning signs

Even when a license is required, there is no guarantee that every contractor you encounter will actually *have* a license. While there are certainly honest and competent contractors out there, the industry is unfortunately plagued with incompetence and con artists. It is essentially up to you to protect yourself. Therefore, when evaluating potential contractors, you should be diligent in your screening process. There are a number of "red flags" you should watch for:

- **Unsolicited phone calls or visits.** Although some reputable contractors market their services in this way, it is a tactic more often used by remodeling con artists. Be especially wary of a contractor who offers you a bargain price, claiming that he or she is doing a job in the neighborhood and has leftover materials.
- **High-pressure sales pitches or scare tactics.** Don't be pushed into hiring a contractor by forceful sales techniques, special "today-only" deals, or the threat that some defect in your house is a safety hazard. Dishonest and disreputable contractors often prey on their victims' fears by warning them that their furnace is about to blow up, their roof is about to collapse, or some similar catastrophe is about to occur.
- **Large down payments**. State law may govern how much money contractors can ask for a deposit on a job. If a contractor asks for too much money up front or insists you pay in cash, it can be a sign that he or she is going to take your money and run.
- **No verifiable address and phone number.** Be cautious of contractors who give you a post office box with no street address or who seem to use only an answering service. According to Oriol Torres, the electrical code compliance officer for Dade County, FL, most home improvement con artists operate without a traceable phone number. "They all use either beepers or cellular phones," he said. "They're very hard to track down that way."
- **Unwillingness to give you a price.** A reputable contractor should be able to provide you with a bid before beginning work on your project. If the contractor says he or she can't do so or skirts the issue of cost, you are at great risk of being taken advantage of.

- **Unwillingness to sign a written contract.** Always get the terms of the construction agreement in writing. A complete contract should include: a description of the work done, materials used, labor cost, timetable, payment schedule, completion date, names of subcontractors, warranty agreements, clean up, and financing arrangements. It should also include the contractor's license number and should address the issues of project cancellation and how overruns on time and cost will be handled.
- **Insurance or licensing information you cannot verify.** A qualified contractor should be able to provide you with proof of both licensing and insurance coverage. If the contractor can't give you a copy of his or her license and insurance policy, have him or her at least give you the license and policy numbers. It is a good idea, also, to ask for some other proof of identification at this time, so you can be sure you are actually dealing with the person whose name appears on the license. Checking the validity of licensing and insurance information is covered below.

Don't rely on a handshake

Familiarize yourself with the licensing requirements for contractors. If you have Internet access, you can find this information online. Two sites that maintain state-by-state contractor licensing information are http://www.contractornet.com and http://www.nationalcontractor.com. The National Association of the Remodeling Industry (NARI) also maintains information on state licensing requirements and a list of state agencies' phone numbers. You can also call your local building or planning department to inquire about licensing requirements.

When you're shopping for contractors, be sure to verify that both the license and insurance information you get are correct. Using the insurance policy number, call the contractor's carrier to make sure the policy is still in effect and that it covers projects such as yours. Also, call your state or local licensing board to verify the contractor's licensing information. The licensing agency should also be able to tell you if there have been any complaints registered against that contractor. You might also call your Consumer Affairs Bureau and Better Business Bureau to ask about any consumer complaints they may have received.

Thirteen Steps to Hiring a Contractor

1. Seek a referral from someone you know who is happy with his or her contractor's work.

2. Solicit bids from at least three contractors.
3. Be wary of proposals that are much lower than any other proposals.
4. Contact the Better Business Bureau to check out any contractors that submit bids.
5. Insist on a written contract that outlines your entire agreement, including starting and completion dates.
6. Have an attorney review any documents before you sign them, including contracts, warranties, and plans.
7. Make sure there are no blank spaces on anything you sign.
8. Insist upon a written warranty on all materials and work.
9. Get all building permits and variances before starting the project, and identify the contractor on the applications.
10. Inspect all work before signing a completion certificate.
11. Withhold final payment until the entire project is finished and inspected.
12. Get a contractor's affidavit that all subcontractors and material suppliers have been paid before making final payment.
13. Report any misrepresentations, shoddy work, failure to honor contracts, unlicensed contractors, or other problems to the appropriate licensing board.

To better your chances of being satisfied with a contractor's work, you can also:

- Ask a recognized construction industry association to recommend a reputable contractor in your area. The National Association of the Remodeling Industry (800-611-NARI (6274),the National Association of Homebuilders (800-368-5242), Associated Builders and Contractors (888-422-2277), or the Associated General Contractors of America (703-548-3118) may all be able to help. Check with neighbors, friends, and relatives who have recently completed a home improvement project to see if they can recommend their contractor.
- Ask local suppliers of building materials, hardware, or appliances if they can recommend a contractor.
- Ask potential contractors for references from people they have worked for in your area. If possible, get photographs of some of their previous projects.
- Get several estimates—at least three—so you can comparison shop.

- Get references on potential contractors from their banks, suppliers, and subcontractors. Any indication of being financially unsound or behind on bills or payments should be taken as a warning sign.
- Check the public records in your local courthouse to see if potential contractors have any liens against them.
- Determine who will actually perform your work. Ask to meet all employees or subcontractors who will be working on your property.
- Establish in advance an agreed-upon process for arbitrating disagreements.

Request a warranty, lasting at least one year from completion date.

- Have an attorney review all contracts or other paperwork before signing anything.

Even after you hire a contractor, your work is not complete. You will still need to remain in close contact with the contractor to ensure the work proceeds on schedule and according to contract. And you may encounter complications or disagreements that need to be ironed out as the project unfolds. However, if you select your contractor carefully in the beginning, you are less likely to have problems later. While screening contractors may seem like more work than the construction project itself, the effort can save enormously in money, annoyance, and time.

Recommendations for the Building Owner When Selecting a Contractor to Perform Work on an Existing Home or to Construct a New Home

Before you enter into any written agreement to construct a new home or to remodel or build an addition onto an existing home:

1. Ensure that the Contractor is appropriately licensed and is a Licensed Construction Supervisor and/or a Registered Home Improvement Contractor.
2. Ensure that the contractor has adequate liability insurance and workers compensation insurance.
3. Ask the contractor for a written list of his or her three most recent projects with names, telephone numbers, and addresses of the owners.

4. Call the owners and ask questions as to the performance of the contractor.

Check with your local Better Business Bureau, the Board of Building Regulations and Standards, and the office of the Attorney General to find out whether the contractor has any complaints filed against the contractor, or whether or not any disciplinary action has been taken against the contractor.

Once you have selected a contractor and before you sign any agreement or contract:

1. Do not enter into any construction agreements without a written contract. Before signing a contract, make sure that your attorney reviews the contract.
2. Ensure that you authorize the contractor to apply for the building permit as your agent.

CHAPTER FOUR
Vacations

Preparing your home

You've worked hard all year. You shoveled snow and cleared sidewalks in the dead of winter. The time has come for a vacation. You have planned for this and can't wait for the fun and excitement of carefree living. Before you leave for your destination, there are a few things you need to do. As covered in chapters 1 and 2, be sure your home is safe from unwanted guests. I mean the two-legged kind that want the goods that you have. I will touch on some of the important points for those who may have skimmed through. (If you are like me, my recall of what I have read is not the greatest.) So here are some of the important steps for preparing your home when you leave, whether for a weekend, two weeks, or even for a season.

The first thing to do is make a list of everything that needs to be checked. As you go through the list, check each item as you inspect your home. After the car is packed and before you make your final exit, check the list again. Be sure to give yourself plenty of time to go through this list. You do not want to rush it and then second-guess yourself a few hours into your trip. There is nothing worse than having to call someone to double check your house after you are gone. Your list might look something like this:

- Check windows to be sure they are locked.
- Make sure sliding door is locked with a wedge in the door track.
- Timers on lights, radio, and maybe the television are set. Be sure all light bulbs are working.

- Forward calls to your cell phone. If this cannot be done and you have an answering machine, be sure you can listen to your messages remotely and do that at least every two or three days if possible. Do not change the message to indicate you are on vacation.
- Either cancel the newspaper or have someone pick it up daily; same thing for mail delivery.
- Put valuables in your safe deposit box.
- Take a good look around the house and be sure nothing can be seen from the outside that thieves may want; if you can see it, so can they.
- Notify the police that you will be on vacation; they usually send a car by occasionally for a visual check.
- If you have a neighbor you can trust, have him or her park a car in the driveway; be sure to let the police know who is parking there.
- Have someone cut the grass or shovel the snow while you are gone.
- Do not have leave the blinds or shades closed. Leave a couple open to make the home look lived in.
- Do not leave any notes on the door.
- Have a close friend or relative come by and check the doors and windows once in a while.

If you have a security system in your home, be sure to notify the company as well. The last thing you should do before you leave is check and make sure the alarm is set and the company knows how to get in touch with you. You may want to have them contact someone you trust in town in case of an emergency. Knowing that your home is well secured will make for a relaxing and carefree vacation.

Protecting yourself

This section will deal with cons and other types of trouble to be aware of, whether while on vacation or when you leave home. You do not have to be traveling to become a victim.

You are poolside at the hotel where you are vacationing, enjoying the sun and maybe some small talk with your spouse. Your wife starts to put some sunscreen on you. A stranger sits next to you and starts a conversation. Just little things like "You missed a spot over there" or "The water was really cold yesterday." Just enough to take your attention away from the purse your wife brought with her because you didn't want to bring your wallet or leave money out in the open. To get away from this person, you both decide to go into the pool. You keep an eye on your things while whispering about the stranger. The purse is still there, and your things look like they have not moved in any way. He leaves, and you get out of the pool and enjoy the sun for a while longer. Then you decide that it is time to get something to eat. You grab your stuff, go to your room, and get ready. The meal was great, just what you expected. Your wife says, "I'll buy dinner and you buy the drinks later." Hey, you don't have to ask me twice. She pulls out her wallet from her purse and looks for her credit cards—they are gone. You both try to think where and when she used them the last time. That morning she used one when she bought a couple gifts for the kids. Then you remember the pool and that irritating guy next to you. Her purse was on ground behind her as she was putting the sunscreen on you. He had an accomplice.

True story. How embarrassing for it to happen to us. Our guard was down. We were having a great time and did not think something like that could happen. I would never have thought of being double-teamed like that. Moral of the story—only take what you need to the pool, nothing more: your room key or card and enough money to get what you need. Charging things to your room may be another way to go. But who can you trust. You give the waiter your room number and sign off for some drinks. The waiter lets a friend know that you are not in your room. Maybe I have seen too many movies. But why take chances?

Men who carry their wallets in their back pockets can become a victim of a pickpocket. Some are so skilled at their art that they can cut the bottom of the pocket with a razor and let the wallet fall out without you even knowing it happened. Guys, carry your wallet in the front pocket. Do not put it in the inside pocket of your sport jacket. Consider carrying the money and your ID in a money clip, again in the front pocket.

Be very selective about who you ask to take your picture. Do you really feel comfortable giving a stranger your camera to take that picture? Most of the time there will not be a problem. Ask yourself: Are you in a foreign country? What are your gut feelings in this part of town? Often you hear stories about the person you ask to take your picture actually taking the camera and running off through the crowd or to a waiting car. So use your better judgment in those situations.

While enjoying the sights, keep your eyes moving. Don't be afraid to make eye contact with anyone. Just a glance can give you a lot of information: height, color of hair, facial hair, scars, and many other traits that could help you identify them if needed. Should you be worried every second on vacation? Certainly not, but making it a habit to be a people-watcher as well as a sightseer may save you a lot of headaches. This practice works as well on vacation as in everyday life. Here is another good example, and although this is meant more for women, men should use this method also. If you feel you are being followed, keep your eyes moving. Never walk with your head down and eyes focused on the ground. This gives off a sense of insecurity and lack of confidence. Keep your head and eyes moving from side to side and watch others walking in the same direction as you as well as those walking toward you to create a better chance of spotting trouble before it happens. Making eye contact is also very important. You do not have to stare anyone down. Brief eye contact gives you an aura of self-confidence. When walking in any business district, look at the reflections in a window to see if someone is following you. You can also look down occasionally at the ground to watch the shadows, if you feel someone is following you, if the sun is behind you. If you think you are being followed, change directions. Cross the street. Go into a store. If you feel this person is still following you, tell an employee at the store. Get the manager, and be sure you know what the person looks like. Be sure to walk on well-lighted streets and stay away from vacant lots, alleys, or construction sites where there may not be any workers when you're passing. If no stores are open and you have changed directions and crossed the street, turn and confront the person. Be sure the person is following you, because what you do next is very important. In a very loud and confident voice say, *"What do you want?"* Most attackers do not want someone who is confrontational, loud, defensive, and aggressive. They are looking for someone who will cower and be quietly afraid. If something does happen, do not yell the word *help.* There have been many instances where people ignore someone being assaulted who yells for help. However, yelling the word *fire* will get a better response. Also, make as much noise as possible to draw attention to yourself and the situation. A loud whistle is also a good thing to use. As for mace or pepper spray, unless you have it in your hand and your finger on the button, with the wind at your back, forget about it.

In chapter 7, I will give some self-defense tips that may help in many assault situations.

CHAPTER FIVE
Driving, Shopping, or Just Out and About

Driving and safety in your vehicle

This chapter has so much to cover I almost don't know where to begin. To start, I believe everyone knows to never, ever, pick up hitchhikers. However, if I did not mention it, I know that this would be brought to my attention.

Usually it is better to have a traveling companion. When shopping, banking, or going to church—anywhere you go—it is a good idea to have someone with you. This becomes more important as we get older. However, this may not always be possible. No one likes to be treated like a child or feel as if you must always tell someone what your plans are for each and every move you make anytime you leave your home. But if you must go alone, whether you are older or living alone, a good idea for most is to write a note on where you were planning to go. You really don't need to go into detail about the route you were going to take or the times you were leaving or going to arrive home. Whether you live alone or you may be the only one home at the time you leave, still leave a note. That way if something happens to you, friends and loved ones have a point from which to start looking. As we get older we feel it is nobody's business where and what we do. We just don't remember that we once worried about our parents and grandparents, just as they worried about us when we were younger. Sometimes just a quick phone call to a child or loved one at work to let them know what you are doing can be helpful.

In our own hometowns, most of us know how to get where we are going. Still, having many things on our minds or if listening to the radio (hope you are not using the cell phone or texting), we could miss a turn or exit. When this occurs, find a gas station or parking lot to turn around in to get back on track. If you are on an interstate, toll road, or any other kind of highway with exits that are miles apart, do not try to make a U-turn. If you pass your exit do not try to back up along the side of the road to the exit. If a detour occurs, drive slowly enough to follow the signs, but do not hold up traffic; keep up with the speed limit. Always stay alert to traffic, oncoming or otherwise. Vehicles coming out of side streets or driveways may present a danger to you if they are not themselves fully aware. Keep your eyes moving, looking for playing children or animals that dart out from between parked or stopped vehicles.

Staying alert, aware, and tuned into your surroundings is a full-time job. Don't daydream. While stopped at red lights or stop signs, keep your eyes moving. This is especially important in unfamiliar neighborhoods. However, you could be right down the street from your home and still become a victim. Never let your gas tank drop below half full. You may have to stop more often for fuel, but you will never run out of gas. This is very important in the colder climates during bad weather. Anytime you stop your vehicle, keep it in gear unless you are ready to exit the vehicle.

Check your four-way emergency flashers to be sure they are operational. This should be done several times a year. At home, put on the flashers and walk around the vehicle to make sure all are operational. You can check your brake lights and directional signals at night, either in the garage or when backed up to any wall. Just by looking in your mirror and applying the brakes, you can see the reflection on the wall. The same goes for the directional signals. Every time I have pulled up to someone with no brake lights and mentioned it to them, they had no idea they were not working. Any time your vehicle breaks down, be wary of strangers who offer to help. Stay in the vehicle, keep the doors locked, and call for help. If you don't have a cell phone and someone stops to help you, ask him or her to call for you, and *do not get out of the vehicle.* If you called for help and someone wants to help you, tell him or her you have already called for help and are waiting for the police and tow truck to arrive. Try to make sure that your vehicle is out of the flow of traffic. If you get a flat tire or your vehicle seems like it is going to stop running, try to move as far to the right side of the road as possible. If you are on the highway in the far left lane and there is room to move left out of traffic, do so. Make sure the passengers and/or animals in the vehicle are safe and under control.

Be sure that anyone approaching your vehicle does so out of harm's way from the traffic. If you must exit your vehicle, do so away from traffic; i.e., on the passenger side. When calling for help, be sure to give the best possible directions about where you are and what type and color of vehicle you have, as well as any other information you think they may need. Try to get an approximate time the help will arrive. If possible, give the type of vehicle trouble you are experiencing. When help arrives, if you have any doubt about whether the person is who they say they are, ask for identification.

You are driving in an unfamiliar area. It does not matter how or why you are in this area—you may just be following a map or your GPS directions that take you through there. Traffic is kind of light; it may be early morning or dusk, but it could be any time of the day. You get to a red light or a stop sign and *bam*. Someone hits you from behind. It doesn't feel like there was a lot of damage. You decide to get out and check your vehicle. This could be the biggest mistake of your life. Many times thieves will use this tactic to rob you and steal your vehicle, or maybe something even worse. Stay in your vehicle and try to get the license plate number and type of vehicle that hit you. Make a police report as soon as possible.

Keep packages, purses, and any valuables out of sight of anyone who may be walking past you while you are stopped. Ladies, if your purse is in the front seat, have the seatbelt looped through the strap or handle. Keep your eyes moving at all times, especially when stopped; this may prevent any smash-and-grab type of crime. Anytime there is a vehicle in front of you, be sure to leave enough distance to pull around them if needed. By checking your mirrors you can keep from being followed or targeted. We touched on this in chapter 1 regarding being followed to your home.

It has been a few days since you had to drive anywhere. You are now on your way to the mall to shop for birthday presents or maybe summer clothes. The destination or reason does not really matter; however, you notice that you need to get some gas. You find the station you usually go to and pull up next to a vacant pump. Your mind wanders, and, boy, that candy bar sounds good about now. Just because you have been to this station many times before, do not let your guard down. Keep your keys in your hand and do not daydream. Keep your eyes moving, look around, and check out the other people and vehicles. Ladies, do not leave your purse unattended in plain sight in the car without locking the door.

When was the last time you checked the panic button on the remote for your car keys? You should check it several times a year. Then if you have a situation where you need it, you can rest assured it will work. If someone approaches you while you are pumping gas, you should be ready with your thumb or finger on the panic button. It does not happen all the time, but there are many cases of someone taking the vehicle from someone right at the gas pump. *Do not leave you vehicle running while you are getting gas!* Aside from the dangers of fire, you may set yourself up for a theft as well.

Great—now the gas tank is full, you have your candy bar or soft drink, and you are ready to get to your destination.

Road Rage

Road Rage Statistics

National auto discount club AutoVantage administered a survey to determine which cities have the most aggressive drivers. AutoVantage polled participants about how their fellow drivers behave on the road. The survey shows that people believe road rage is usually the result of triggers like feeling rushed, speeding, or being in traffic. Other aggressive driving behaviors include tailgating, changing lanes without using a signal, talking on cell phones while driving, running red lights, honking the horn, and using angry or obscene gestures at other drivers. Participants also provided suggestions on how to decrease road-rage incidents. Suggestions ranged from outlawing talking on a cell phone while driving to increasing police presence on the roads. Only 32 percent of the respondents felt that a major public awareness campaign would be useful. Psychologist Dr. Leon James argues that extensive driver's education courses beginning at grade-school level are necessary to decrease road-rage incidents.

So where in the United States are you going to find the most aggressive drivers? According to the survey, that dubious honor belongs to Miami, FL. Miami has a very diverse, dense population, including a large community of senior citizens who have a very different driving style from younger drivers. The other four cities rounding out the top five include New York City, Boston, Los Angeles, and Washington, DC. The city with the most courteous drivers was Portland, OR. Pittsburgh, Seattle/Tacoma, St. Louis, and Dallas/Fort Worth also ranked high in driver courtesy.

Statistically, young men are the most prone to road rage. Whether this is due to a predisposition to aggression, a lack of experience, or just the simple fact that young men tend to drive more than other age and gender groups is still a subject of debate. In a 2002 Rage-Depression Survey, the most competitive, aggressive population polled was men under the age of 19.

Men reported feeling a sense of rage more frequently than women. Fifty-six percent of the men surveyed said they experienced rage on a daily basis versus 44 percent of the women. More men also admitted to retaliating against others when they felt angry or provoked.

Recently, several writers have published articles about the rise in road-rage incidents among women. Most of these articles are written from an editorial perspective, with few facts or figures to support observations. However, there is the perception that women are closing the aggression gap.

It's important to keep in mind that road rage isn't some uncontrollable phenomenon. As drivers, we each have the responsibility to be as safe as we can. We also each have the choice over whether to engage in aggressive behaviors or retaliate against a real or perceived insult. So the next time you're driving and someone cuts you off or honks at you, try to keep a cool head and set a good example.

Introduction to How Road Rage Works

Road rage became a popular buzz term in the 1990s, as stories about motorists attacking one another in parking lots and intersections seemed to increase.

So what do you think of when you hear the term *road rage*? It's one of those catch phrases everyone has heard, and yet there is no common definition we can all use. Often, people use terms like *road rage* and *aggressive driving* interchangeably. And while some might say that aggressive driving includes everything from cutting someone off on purpose to tailgating to making obscene gestures and cursing at other drivers, others might claim road rage refers only to incidents where violence erupts between drivers and passengers— in or around cars. (There are just as many who might reverse those two definitions.) One thing is certain—road rage is a dangerous phenomenon that can happen to any one of us, either as a perpetrator or a victim.

In most jurisdictions, road rage isn't a specific crime. Many aggressive driving maneuvers fall under the category of traffic violations, but there are only a few districts that try to define aggressive driving or road rage as an illegal activity. One reason most states don't classify road rage as a crime is that lawmakers often find it difficult to quantify road-rage behaviors. For example, a law might state that it's illegal to follow a car too closely. But what is too close and who makes that determination? Without providing specific parameters, the law is completely subjective.

[For the purposes of this article,] we'll look at road rage in the broadest spectrum, from driving aggressively to violent confrontations between drivers. We'll examine the psychology behind road rage, common behaviors associated with road rage, ways to avoid getting into confrontations with angry drivers, and how to determine and alleviate your own road rage. We'll also look at some statistics on road rage, including which cities have the most aggressive drivers.

Road Rage Mindset

Driving a car is stressful—it's inherently dangerous because even if you're the safest driver in the world, there are a lot different variables that you can't predict, like weather, traffic, accidents, and road work. And what about all those other people on the road? Some of them aren't just bad drivers, they're engaging in risky behavior. Some of them even do things specifically to make you angry or prevent you from getting to where you need to go. That's the thought progression someone might have just before switching into road-rage mode, leading a driver to make irrational decisions very quickly. All of a sudden, you might be thinking: They need to know that what they're doing is dangerous and stupid, and you should show them. In fact, you should punish them. There's no denying that driving can be a risky and emotional experience. For many of us, our cars are an extension of our personality, and it might be the most expensive possession we own. When we drive, we're aware that there's potential for injury and property damage. Driving might be an expression of freedom for some, but it's also an activity that tends to increase our stress levels, even if we're not aware of it at the time. Driving is also a communal activity. You might think of driving in terms of your own individual experience. But once you pull into traffic, you've joined a community of other drivers, all of whom have their own goals, fears, and driving skills. Psychologists Dr. Leon James and Dr. Diane Nahl say that one factor in road rage is our tendency to concentrate on ourselves while dismissing the communal aspect of driving. It's very easy to perceive another driver's actions in terms of how it affects us, which in turn makes it easy to transition into anger.

Unleashing Your Inner Alligator

Neurologist Paul MacLean proposes that the human mind is the combination of three brains, one of which is known as the *reptilian brain* and is similar to the brain found in reptiles. This part of the human mind, which consists of the brainstem and cerebellum, is responsible for our sense of survival and the fight-or-flight reaction we have to fear and stress. Road-rage incidents stem from the stimulation of the reptilian mind. A driver experiencing road rage feels threatened and responds aggressively to ensure survival. MacLean states that the reptilian brain is inflexible, compulsive, ritualistic, and incapable of learning from previous experience.

Once an expert witness to Congress on traffic psychology, Dr. James, known as "Dr. Driving," believes that the core cause of road rage isn't due to traffic jams or more drivers on the road, but how our culture views aggressive driving. In our culture, children learn that the normal rules regarding behavior and civility don't apply when driving a car. They may see their parents engage in competitive-driving behaviors, maneuvering the car with multiple lane changes or traveling at high speeds in a rush to get to a destination. Some popular films and television shows portray aggressive driving as a positive, or at the very least, an exciting activity.

To complicate matters, pop psychologists suggested that the best way to relieve anger and stress was to vent your frustration, essentially giving into and feeding your negative emotions. However, psychological studies show that venting doesn't help relieve anger at all. In a road-rage situation, venting can help escalate an incident into a violent encounter. Americans also tend to view a person who backs away from confrontation as a coward, creating a sense of pressure on a driver to not give up any ground even when no one is judging him. With that in mind, it's no surprise that violent encounters happen occasionally. Almost everyone is predisposed to engaging in irrational behavior while driving. Dr. James even goes so far as to say that most people are emotionally impaired when they drive. The key, psychologists say, is being aware of your emotional state and making the right choices, even when you are tempted to act out emotionally.

Anatomy of a Road Rage Incident

A typical road-rage incident happens when at least one driver chooses to act out in anger. Usually, the driver is already feeling stress when something triggers an aggressive reaction. Many road-rage drivers reported being under duress in other areas of their lives, like work or relationships, all of which contribute to a driver's stress level, making him more vulnerable to engaging in irrational behavior. Dr. James also identifies several aspects of driving that contribute to our frustration and stress levels, including:

- **Immobility.** We're stuck sitting behind the steering wheel and can't physically relieve tension.
- **Constriction.** Because we must drive on roads, our options are limited, often giving us the feeling of being boxed in.
- **Lack of control.** Although we maintain control of our own vehicle, many other variables, like traffic, lane closures, and the behavior of other drivers, are completely outside of our influence.
- **Territoriality.** Like many animals, human beings react negatively when we feel our space is threatened by someone else.
- **Denial and loss of objectivity.** We tend to overlook our own faults and place blame on others.
- **Unpredictability.** We all know that every time we drive there are going to be unexpected events, such as someone pulling out into traffic ahead of you without warning—this makes driving more stressful.
- **Ambiguity.** Because there's no culturally agreed-upon way to signal an apology to another driver, it's easy to misinterpret someone's actions as a sign of aggression or insult.

Many police incident reports mention that multiple parties contributed to the escalation of emotions leading up to a violent encounter. As one driver reacts in anger to the other, the second driver in turn reacts negatively, and the emotions (and aggressive tactics) escalate, feeding each other in a vicious cycle. Ultimately, these behaviors lead to a complete surrender to base emotional reactions, and the drivers leave rationality behind.

Dan Goleman, a psychologist who coined the term *Emotional Intelligence*, says that anger is a seductive emotion. When you get angry, your heart beats faster and your body prepares for confrontation. The rush of adrenaline that comes as a result of real or perceived danger makes it easy for us to give into anger. It's a real challenge to impose self-control and behave in a way that's contradictory to how you initially feel. In other words, road rage tends to happen because it's easy to fall into the trap of directing anger toward another driver.

Road Rage or Aggressive Driving?

One of the big issues with aggressive driving and road rage is that the driving public and the police define *aggressive* very differently. Surveys show that many drivers don't consider certain behaviors, like honking the car horn or changing lanes without signaling, to be aggressive at all. One survey found that only 47 percent of American drivers consider driving ten miles per hour over the speed limit to be a kind of aggressive driving, though law enforcement officials tend to disagree [source: Dr. Driving.org]. There's a wide range of aggressive-driving behaviors, some of which are potentially much more dangerous than others. Dr. James divides aggressive driving into three areas: impatience and inattentiveness, power struggles, and recklessness and road rage.

- **Impatience and inattentiveness.** These can be categorized by behaviors like driving through red lights, rolling through stop signs, blocking intersections, speeding, and not using signals when turning or changing lanes. Drivers who engage in these behaviors often say that their schedules are very busy, that they've run out of time, or that their mind was on something else. This is the lowest level of aggressive-driving behaviors that are annoying and could trigger road rage in another but are less risky than other negative behaviors.
- **Power struggles.** These are more serious, and they include preventing someone from moving over into your lane, using gestures or obscene language to humiliate or threaten other drivers, tailgating and cutting off another driver, or braking without warning as an act of retaliation. These behaviors stem from an unhealthy mentality in which drivers feel as if they're the target of malicious acts. Many people feel a sense of entitlement and self-righteousness when behind the wheel of a car. It's common for them to feel that someone who makes a mistake needs to be punished. Most of us have wished for another driver to feel guilt or shame for an action we've deemed stupid or dangerous. According to Dr. James, that's the first step to entering into a power struggle.
- **Recklessness and road rage.** The most serious incidents include behaviors like entering into a duel with another car, racing at dangerous speeds, and committing assault with a weapon or your vehicle. In these cases, aggressive driving gives way to outright violence. While road rage isn't exactly a worldwide epidemic, studies have shown that incidents have increased each

year. Skeptics point out that this could be due to an increase in reporting incidents, however, and may not actually indicate an increase in cases.

Avoiding Road Rage

Here's the bad news: everyone makes mistakes, even you. No matter how skilled a driver you are, you're bound to make an error at some point that could seriously agitate another driver. Here's some news that's worse: sometimes you don't even have to make a mistake to trigger someone else's road rage. Because a person experiencing road rage isn't rational, he might interpret a reaction as innocent as an increase in speed as an act of aggression. Fortunately, there's some good news to go along with the bad. By keeping a level head and calm point of view, you can avoid most conflicts:

- Don't show a physical reaction to an aggressive driver's behavior. In particular, you should avoid eye contact, as this is often seen as a sign of mutual aggression. Advice like this might give you the impression that drivers experiencing road rage are similar to aggressive animals in the wild. According to some psychologists, that might not be too far off.
- It's very important to keep control of your own temper when someone is driving aggressively. Remember that many people don't view their own actions as aggressive. Surveys have shown that drivers often think of their own actions as assertive but not aggressive. Try not to match another driver's behavior.
- Don't use your car horn to express displeasure at other drivers— doing so might make them more aggressive. It's extremely difficult to resist the urge to express yourself. Individual expression has deep roots in our culture, and to deny yourself that venue seems counterintuitive and unnatural. Try to keep in mind that there are more important factors than your displeasure. Remember that your safety, the safety of your vehicle, and the safety of everyone around you is far more important than your sense of indignation.

Try to be kind and courteous to your fellow drivers. The best way to avoid road rage is to practice good driving habits. When you do encounter an aggressive driver, it's better to let him have his way, even when it feels unfair. It's easy to think of this as letting the bad guy win, but try to avoid that mentality. It's more important to think of driving as a group experience instead of a competition. Try to increase the distance between you and the aggressive driver. Remember that he is likely under just as much stress as you are—he's just really bad at handling it.

Preventing Road Rage

So how do we avoid becoming a road warrior? It requires both a stronger focus on our driving habits and a shift in our attitude toward driving. There are some specific things you can do to help reduce your vulnerability to giving in to road rage, but the bottom line is that it takes commitment.

Road Rage and Health

Road-rage incidents can escalate to full-blown, violent encounters ending in tragedy, but even just getting angry can be bad for your health. Dr. Leon James says that giving into anger releases stress hormones, which can overtax your heart and circulatory system [source: BBC News].

Here are some building blocks you can use to help avoid going off the deep end while driving your car:

- Make sure you're getting enough sleep. Driving without enough rest can make you more irritable and dangerous.
- Try to give yourself plenty of time to get to where you're going. Often, frustrations bubble up when we feel we're running out of time, especially in traffic. Another strategy is to accept that you're running late, and you can't do anything about it.
- Listen to relaxing music and concentrate on breathing. Try to avoid aggressive thoughts and concentrate on something neutral instead. The more you focus on a trigger, the more likely you'll make yourself angry.
- Don't show displeasure to other drivers. There's a good chance that whatever has ticked you off was a mistake on the other driver's part. It's very unlikely the other driver is singling you out, and even if he is, it's not worth it to follow suit. So resist the urge to honk your horn, curse, and go through the array of obscene gestures in your repertoire.
- Avoid venting. It isn't helpful and can actually increase your elevated sense of danger and frustration. There's also the chance that the driver will see you and react in kind, escalating the situation. As difficult as it may seem, it's better to avoid venting

your frustrations. Instead, assume the driver doesn't mean to be unsafe or thoughtless [source: Dr. Driving.org].

Self-assessment and self-control are key components to keeping your cool. First, you have to recognize the moment you have a choice whether or not to act in anger. Then you have to develop the willpower to choose not to indulge in negative behavior. Dr. James says that such a change may take a long time and involves changing perspectives about other drivers as much as it does changing your own driving behavior. [5]

Just input *road rage* into your search engine. There you will find many other articles on this subject. The previous information seemed to be most informative to this author.

Parking your vehicle

You have managed to get to your destination—the mall, the bank, wherever you were going. Now you need to find a parking spot. If you have a handicap permit, there usually is no problem finding a spot. Be sure and try to choose a well-lit, well-traveled area. If it is dark when you arrive or when you will be leaving, always check for lighting. Let's use the mall as an example; it happens to be a busy time for them. When you exit your vehicle there are many thoughts going on inside your head, such as what stores to go to, where they are located inside the mall, prices, etc. However, looking for some type of identifying marks to relocate where we parked is usually not one of them. Choose your parking spot wisely; always be aware of where you parked and who and what is around you. Do not park between two large vehicles, such as large vans or trucks. If you must park between them, be sure to glance inside them before exiting your car. You never know what kind of person is inside or what their intentions may be. If you feel at all uneasy, go to a different parking spot. Make it a habit to lock the doors. When using the remote to lock the doors, you can also set the alarm for the vehicle. If you are unsure whether it is locked, try to open the door. If you do not have a remote to lock up, be sure that all the doors are locked before exiting, then lock your door and check to be sure it is locked. If you have shopped elsewhere and have packages, be sure they are in the trunk or well out of sight from those who may be looking to break into vehicles.

When shopping, always wear comfortable clothes and shoes. You do not have to dress to the nines to shop. Wear clothing and shoes that do not restrict your

5   Road Rage HowStuff Works, Inc. © 1998–2009

movement. Do not wear expensive jewelry when shopping, or even going to work. Think about this the next time you wear jewelry to work or to shop. You may be going to and from a safe area; however, a car accident or car trouble can put you in a vulnerable position. Working in a customer service job, such as working in a restaurant, convenience store, or any number of customer service jobs, and wearing expensive jewelry can make you a target. While shopping, this will do nothing but make you a target for some thief who happens to want what you are wearing. Take only what you need as far as credit cards are concerned. One would be preferable. When paying in cash, do not pull out a wad of bills while in line. If you carry a large sum of money (20s, 50s or 100s) folded in half, be sure to have the larger bills in the middle of the stack surrounded by the smaller bills (1s and 5s). Ladies, with cash, count your money inside your purse. Speaking of which, try to carry a small purse. Ladies, try carrying a small change purse with only the money or credit cards that you need, instead of a large handbag with straps. And guys, keep your wallet in an inside jacket pocket or front pants pocket.

Do not burden yourself with packages. If you intend to purchase many items, have someone go shopping with you. When shopping at various locations, do not leave packages in plain sight. And it cannot be said often enough—always put packages in the trunk. Be sure the doors are locked and the alarm is set.

Many prey on shoppers they think will be easy targets. Often they use a simple ploy, such as, "Excuse me, did you drop that …?" Maybe money, a credit card or maybe even a set of keys. Do not fall for it, as they are probably sizing you up for a quick grab and run. They may want your purse or packages. This type of con is commonly employed against the elderly and women shopping alone. Thieves usually use an accomplice to run interference for them in case the victim or someone else tries to run after them or stop them.

Whether you are shopping in a mall or a freestanding store, always walk in a confident, relaxed manner. Do not be afraid to make eye contact with people. Walking with your head down, looking at the ground, gives off an aura of lack of confidence. The same can be said if you clutch your purse as if it were a life preserver. Making brief eye contact with approaching strangers gives you a chance to identify them later if needed. Notice height, hair color, scars, and the clothing they wear. You do not have to observe everything—just enough to be able to give some type of description. Trust your instincts. If you feel uncomfortable or uneasy in a store or other situation, do not hesitate to leave. If you feel someone is following you in a store and you want to leave, most stores will send some type of security to escort you to your vehicle. All malls have some type of security, as do most freestanding stores. Try to avoid shopping or walking alone, especially at night. If you must go out at night, see if you can get a friend to accompany you.

Upon returning to your vehicle, take a quick look inside before getting in to be sure there is no one inside. Before you get into your car take a look into the back seat area. Also, if you return to your car and a van or large truck is parked next to you, take a quick peek inside. If you feel unsafe, or if there is someone in the vehicle next to yours that looks suspicious, you can go back inside the mall and have security escort you to your car. No matter if you are backing out or pulling forward to leave the parking spot, proceed slowly and listen for oncoming traffic.

If you notice someone is following you as you are walking to your car, follow you gut feelings. It is better to be cautious than take unnecessary chances. If you feel someone is following you to your car, a simple way to play it safe is to look right past the person and shout something to the effect of, *"Hey George, remember? We are parked over here!"* As you say this, move your arms like you are waving to someone to come over your way. This gives the impression you are not alone.

What should you do if someone tries to force you into your car. If you are approached at your vehicle and they try to force you into the vehicle, throw your keys as far as you can in one direction and run as fast as you can the other way. Some type of self-defense training may give you the skills to strike the eyes, throat, groin, or any other vital area. The last chapter of the book will deal with specific self-defense techniques, such as disabling strikes against your opponent meant to disrupt any one or a combination of the following: balance, breathing, and/or vision. Caution: *do not try these moves without additional training from an experienced qualified instructor at a reputable school.* The techniques in this book give you an idea of what to look for when shopping for the proper training.

Many ideas in this and previous chapters can be used in different situations. Shopping tips can be used at home as well as on vacation. The same can be said for driving tips. Every case is unique in its own way, and only you can make that split-second decision about how it should be handled. Staying alert and aware of everything around you is becoming a full-time job. However, review ideas in this book from time to time and remind yourself to always be on guard, and safety should become second nature.

Chapter Six
Public Transportation and Outdoor Activities

Whether you are traveling on vacation, to work, or just shopping, if you take the bus, subway, train, or other type of public transportation, you need to keep some things in mind.

Using busy and well-lighted stops can make your experience more pleasurable and safe. While you are waiting alone for any type of public transportation, keep your eyes moving. Avoid looking scared, panicked, or otherwise frightened. Fear will surely attract attention from the wrong type of people. If you are standing and waiting, stand close to a utility pole, fence, or anything solid that you can use for balance if needed. Before entering or leaving a vehicle, be sure of your footing. Check the ground to make sure you will not slip or trip on the pavement. Even if there has been no foul weather, something might have spilled or dropped on the ground that could cause you to lose your balance and fall, spraining you ankle or causing some other type of injury. These types of injuries could take many months to heal.

If you are at a crowded boarding station and the vehicles doors start to close before you get on, do not try and force your way in. If the vehicle is too crowded to board safely, be patient and wait for the next one to arrive. Riding an overcrowded vehicle is dangerous and unsafe; it also puts you in the path of pickpockets and other types of unsavory people. When the vehicle arrives, stand to one side and let the exiting passengers get off first. This is not only for you safety, but it is also a common courtesy. Before entering the vehicle, be sure to have proper fare in hand if at all possible. Do not fumble around with cash if there are suspicious people around you. Having the fare ready when you board the vehicle will also help you keep your balance. As you enter a bus, subway, or any type of train system, be sure to watch your step off the curb or platform. Do not be in a hurry. Once on board, remain alert; prepare yourself for when the vehicle begins to move to prevent loss of balance or even a fall, whether you are seated or you must stand for part of or the entire time you are in transit.

If you need to cross the street to gain access to the transportation you need, be sure to allow yourself ample time to so this safely. This is especially true in bad weather. Foul weather makes it harder to see someone crossing the street. Often people trying to catch the bus that is pulling up to the stop do not take the time to check traffic for their own safety. Rain, snow, or any bad weather makes this situation worse for the pedestrian. Traveling at night is a whole different situation. What you wear may save your life. When en route, try to wear fluorescent or light-colored clothing. Shining a flashlight will make it easier for the drivers of other vehicles to see you and also help you identify others if the street lighting is insufficient. A flashlight will help prevent you from twisting your ankle because it was too dark to see a small hole in the sidewalk or a rise in the sidewalk. A flashlight may also be used as a weapon if needed. However, never try to use anything as a weapon that you have not trained with. In chapter 7 and in the video, you can see the ways various items may be used to protect yourself.

When you ride in any public vehicle, such as a taxi or any other that may have a seat belt, use them as you would in your own vehicle. Many times we assume that when we ride on public transportation, we do not need to use seat belts. Do not use time on any public transportation to catch up on your sleep or read a book. Any time you let your guard down you make yourself an easy target. Stay alert at all times. Become a people-watcher. When you enter the vehicle, quickly scan the people that are riding with you. Try to sit close to the driver, not the exit doors. If there are no seats near the driver, but the back does not look as safe as you would like, you can always stand. Always try to sit in an aisle seat. You do not want to be blocked in if you need to exit in a hurry. Do not take any chances. Pay close attention to those who get on after you at the different stops. You do not have to stare; just a quick glance should do the trick. Be a people-watcher and avoid acting nervous; you should be able to keep your eyes moving and analyze your surroundings. Holding on to your purse, briefcase, or other belongings with a death grip will indicate fear and make you a target, as some people feed on fear. Just hold your things securely and comfortably. Do not burden yourself with too many packages and other items. If you need to purchase many items and do not drive, do not take public transportation. Arrange for someone to give you a ride, or call a taxi for the trip home.

As when shopping, wear comfortable shoes and clothing and keep the jewelry to a minimum. Acting confident and not shy is a great deterrent. If you display self-confidence, others will respect you; this is a good deterrent also. If at any time you feel threatened or uncomfortable while in route, let the driver know. They have communication with the transit police or local police department. If you have a cell phone, you can call the local police yourself and explain the situation. When you exit, if you feel threatened by someone who exited with you, try to get back on and go to the next stop; make the driver aware of the situation. If you cannot get back on, stay alert, do not panic, and be prepared to defend yourself (see chapter 7).

Outdoor exercise, jogging, or walking

Today we are far more aware of our physical fitness than ever before. Many of us love the outdoors and the activities we can do to keep in shape: jogging, walking, bicycling … the list goes on and on. Many of us use this time to reflect on our problems, ideas for the future, and many other things. Any such activities done in the inner city or suburbs usually happen on streets that can be very busy. Others prefer to use the park systems for their exercise. The dangers there can include motor vehicle, pedestrian, and even animal attacks. In this section we will try to deal with as many of these dangers as possible.

First and most importantly, always know the route you will be using. It is also helpful to know where and how to get help if needed. Most of us now have cell phones and usually do not leave home without one. For those who may not have one, try to pick a route in which there is a public pay phone. Finding a pay phone is becoming rare these days; I doubt there will any left in a few years. However, if you do need help, find a house where someone is home and have him or her call 911. As mentioned before, let someone know where, when, and what you are doing. Figure out where you want to start and finish before you leave your home. You do not need to call someone every time you go out to exercise; just leave a note at home if no one is there or if you live alone. Along with your cell phone, bring a loud whistle or some other type of device to alert others that you are or may be in trouble. Always have some type of identification with you. There are new devices coming out all the time for just this purpose: an arm band pouch, fanny pack, even a pocket in your workout clothes to hold your ID, blood type or any other medical information, and a phone number in case of an emergency. Do not wear any jewelry or carry any more cash than you absolutely need. Wear clothing that includes some reflective material. Keep your eyes moving.

I know I am repeating some of these safety points; however, some of the safety tips only mentioned once may not sink in as intended. The more alert you are, the less chance you have of becoming a victim. As I mentioned earlier, if you have a dog for home protection, depending on its size, training, and demeanor, they make a great personal defensive weapon when you walking or jogging. A workout partner is also a great idea. Whether you are alone or with someone else, steer clear of unused or overgrown paths. Stay in populated, well-traveled areas, and avoid vacant lots or deserted streets. If you are out after dusk, stay in well-lit areas, carry a flashlight, and be sure to dress appropriately in light-colored, reflective clothing. Try to stay away from tall bushes. If going past parked vehicles, especially trucks and vans, keep a safe distance between you and the vehicle. When approaching someone, whether they are going in the same direction or the opposite direction, make brief eye contact. Learn to sum up his or her stats at a glance: height, weight, noticeable marks, including scars and tattoos. The more you practice this skill, the easier it becomes. If you are using a road or sidewalk in the city, watch where you are going. Always jog or walk against the traffic, even when using the sidewalk. Pay attention to vehicles that may pass you slowly or more than once in a short period of time. Learn to identify the different types of vehicles and work your memory in case you need to remember a license plate number. Look at the ground to be sure of your footing. You need to check the ground for broken glass, raised or uneven pavement or sidewalks, or other hazards that may cause you to slip, trip, or otherwise injure yourself. Checking the ground should only take a few moments.

You should devote most of your time to scanning oncoming traffic, approaching people, people in their yard or in parking lots, and the like. Do not daydream. Beware of vacant lots or construction sites. If you cannot see what is on the other side, tall fences could pose a problem. Stay clear of groups of people you do not know. If you feel uncomfortable upon sizing up a group and you have to cross the street or reverse and go back in the direction from which you came to avoid them, do so before you approach them.

Some of us feel the need to have music or talk radio to listen to as this helps the time pass. If you must use ear buds or headphones, keep the sound turned down so you can hear approaching people, cars, or animals. Listening to loud music will divert your attention from the most important factor—safety—when you are alone. Everyone wants to have a fun and enjoyable workout.

Returning home *safe* is most important of all. Even listening to music with the sound low can and will distract you. Once you know the risks, only you can make the correct decision.

CHAPTER SEVEN
Self-Defense

I must make it clear that in order to become proficient and confident when defending yourself, you must get proper training from a qualified, experienced instructor at a reputable school. *Do not attempt to learn and master the moves in this book and DVD, or any other books or DVDs.* There is no substitute for the insight and knowledge you will receive from a qualified, experienced instructor.

The techniques used in this book are those taught in the Tracy's Kenpo Karate System. As with any martial art, there are many definitive moves to learn in order to progress in the system. These moves are choreographed to make it easier to teach the student, as the moves remain the same from instructor to instructor and school to school.

In self-defense situations, the decisions you will have to make are not very easy and must be made in a split second. You can easily cause permanent damage to someone when choosing certain targets. I have modified the techniques presented here based on the fact that you are not trying to progress through the belt system as in a school or studio. However, the moves will be similar enough to the original technique that if you get training from a studio that teaches the Tracy's system, there will be very few changes to deal with.

Most techniques call for primary and secondary targets to strike; this will give you options based on whether you need to do serious damage to the opponent or just stop someone from being stupid. Primary targets can and usually will cause serious and sometimes long-term injury. Secondary targets may be used if there is no need to cause serious damage to your opponent. Some secondary target examples: instead of using an eye spear to affect the vision, use a palm strike to the face; instead of striking the throat to affect the breathing, use a punch to the chest, face, or mid-section.

The techniques shown are not meant as the one and only way to defend yourself, but they give you an idea of what will be involved when the time comes to protect yourself or a loved one. Always remember that techniques are suggestions and points of reference, not rules. Different combinations are limited only by one's ability and individuality. This is not a game or a sport. If you need to use any type of self-defense, this means you have already exhausted all other means of defusing the situation and you must now take action to keep yourself safe. Make no mistake about what is being taught. First and foremost—only use these moves when absolutely necessary. No one wants to blind, cripple, or kill someone just for being stupid or making a fool of themselves. However, if you feel that your life or physical well-being is in danger, that is when you would use the targets and strikes as they are meant to be used. It is very important to practice *with* someone, not *on* someone. In other words, while practicing be sure not to injure the person helping you. As for the person helping you, be sure he or she reacts as if actually being struck with the weapon (hand strike, elbow, kick, etc.) in the targeted area. This way you will be able to see other targets open up as he or she reacts. Remember that to make any technique successful you need to disrupt the opponent's balance, breathing, or vision. The more disruptions you can accomplish, the greater your success. But first I would like to give a brief history of Kenpo Karate.

Brief History of the Tracy's System of Kenpo Karate

Grand Master Ed Parker opened his first Kenpo karate school in the mainland United States in the mid 1950s. However, the founder of Kenpo karate was not Ed Parker but rather his instructor, Professor William K. S. Chow, who began calling his system Kenpo karate in 1949. Chow trained in Kenpo Jiu-Jitsu under Great Grand Master James Mitose, who had learned the Kenpo art in Japan from his grandfather Sakuhi Yoshida. Three of Mr. Parker's students were brothers, Al, Jim, and Will Tracy. After training under Master Parker and teaching for him at his school, the brothers set out on their own, with the idea that if you teach the students one on one, the student will learn faster and comprehend better. Today there are over 1,500 schools and clubs teaching the Tracy's Kenpo system of karate. In 1969 Hugh Alford, one of Al Tracy's black belts, opened a school in Parma Heights, Ohio. In 1972 Mark Miller bought the school from him and remains at the same location, still teaching today. I started my training in January 1974 under Master Miller. This makes only five generations from Master Chow to me. For more information on the history of Kenpo or any other style, check the related websites.

Basic Stances

Just like when learning play a musical instrument or game, you must start with the basics. When you need to defend yourself, a solid foundation is necessary to maintain your balance and create stability, as well as maximize your power. Terminology is important so we can communicate on the same level.

I will describe three basic stances in this chapter; all the other stances will derive from them. We will start with the horse stance, also called the square horse (see fig. 1). Some systems name this a saddle stance, but it is the same thing. The horse stance dates back two to three thousand years and is used in all forms of judo and karate. Start with your feet slightly more than shoulder-width apart. Bend your knees and push the knees outward, keeping your back straight. This will create a solid foundation for you to work from and will help you maintain your balance. You may practice blocks and punches from this stance, but never fight someone from the horse stance. Many of the self-defense techniques that are taught will use the horse stance.

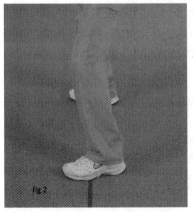

Next we will work the side horse (see fig. 2). At this point it is important to understand *center line*. A center line is an invisible line between you and your opponent. In fig. 2, the tape on the floor represents the center line. In a side horse stance, you are in a horse stance with both feet on the center line, feet apart and knees bent; your side is toward the opponent. The side horse will be used in many techniques as well.

In a fighting stance, also called rear horse (see fig. 3), your front foot, closest to the opponent, will be on one side of the center line and the back foot will be on the other side of the center line. You will adjust hand positioning to your own comfort, but start with something to keep you protected, as in fig. 3. Hand position is only important as described in the individual technique.

fig 3

Self-Defense Techniques

I will name the techniques taught in the Tracy's system. This makes it easier for both the student to learn and the instructor to teach. I will name the move, then in parenthesis tell you what type of attack it is against, followed by a step-by-step definition of the technique. The first technique is knee of vengeance. The idea behind this move is to teach how to strike targets on various parts of the opponent's body using parts of your body.

Knee of Vengeance (*two-handed shirt grab from the front*)

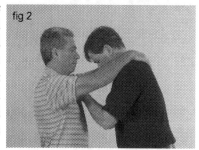
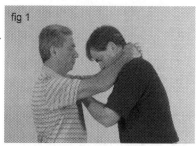

fig 1

fig 2

- Grab with both hands behind opponent's neck (see fig. 1). If unable to grab behind the neck, you can grab the shoulders by going on top (see fig. 2) and behind the shoulder; you can grab the upper arms of the opponent or their clothing. Bring your right knee up to the groin or mid-section as you pull the opponent down and toward you (see fig. 3). Be sure to lean your upper body to the left slightly so you do not get a head butt if the opponent falls toward you after the knee strike. This is all done in one movement.

fig 3

• Stomp on the opponent's nearest foot. Note: if you have the opportunity to rake the shin on the way to the foot stomp or catch the knee cap on the way down as well, this will do more damage to the opponent (see fig. 4 & 5).

• Finish with a right horizontal forearm strike to the left side of the opponent's jaw hinge area (see fig. 6), using the left hand on the right side of the head to trap the head and keep it from moving for maximum effect. The technique as it is normally taught is now complete.

• If you are left-handed, use your left knee and left forearm.

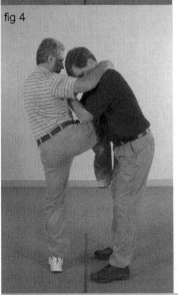

fig 4

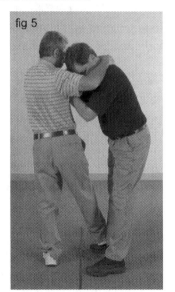

fig 5

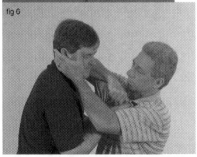

fig 6

Remember that at any point during the execution of this technique you can stop the attack. When young children are taught this move to use against someone their own age, I tell them to push the opponent away after either the knee or the foot stomp. If the opponent drops to the ground after the knee strike, the rest is not necessary. When you are sure the opponent will not continue to attack, leave the area.

Take note of what Knee of Vengeance is teaching you. It teaches to strike different parts of the body, using different weapons. The groin or mid-section, shin to the foot, side of the head, and jaw area are all good targets in different areas of the body. The knee, the sides of the foot and heel, and the forearm are all effective weapons when used properly. Now we are aware that this technique is a defensive move, let's look outside of the box.

I very seldom encourage anyone to be the aggressor or use this material outside of self-defense. However, there are circumstances when you must be the aggressor: for instance, if an opponent approaches along with a few friends and becomes verbally abusive. This person does not place their hands on you or attack you physically, but you feel your physical well-being is in danger. This technique can then be used as an offensive move; however, remember only in the most extreme situations would you ever do so. With more than one person in a dangerous situation, usually there is a leader or loudmouth instigator. If you take this person out quickly and decisively, you will prove you don't fear and have an ability to dispense with them in a manner they may want to avoid.

Again, I must emphasize the importance of proper training and practice. Practice does not make perfect; only perfect practice makes perfect.

The next three techniques will deal with different types of chokes, both from the front and back. Just remember, these are just exercises, ideas, and points of reference, not the only way to stop an opponent. Each system presents one way to deal with an attacker.

Crash of the Eagle *(two-handed rear choke)*
In this situation the opponent is not being aggressive, i.e. not forcing you forward when he starts to choke you from behind.

- Take a deep step back with the right leg to six o'clock between

fig 1

the opponent's feet; lift your right arm up as high as you can (see fig. 1); turn your body to face five o'clock, and then bring your right arm down to the side of your right ribs (see fig. 2); put your

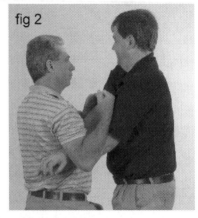
fig 2

left hand on the opponent's upper right arm to control it (see fig. 3), all in one fast, powerful movement. Bring your right arm up as if you are going to scratch your back, striking the opponent with an upward vertical elbow (see fig. 4). Note: It is very important to keep your left hand on the opponent's arm (see fig. 3) while delivering the elbow strike. If the strike is forceful

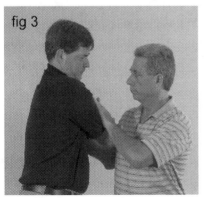
fig 3

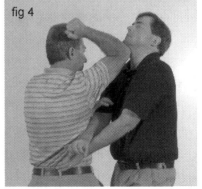
fig 4

enough, he or she may fall back; if you do not have the arm checked, it might strike you during the fall. There are several different endings to this technique. If the opponent's head is facing upward, finish with a downward claw. Bend your wrist back and strike the bridge of the nose with your palm and let

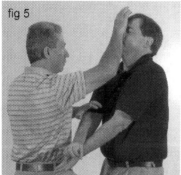

fig 5

your fingers rake along the eye and face (see fig. 5). If the opponent's head is still facing you, finish with a chop to the neck (see fig. 6); anywhere from the base of the skull down the side of the

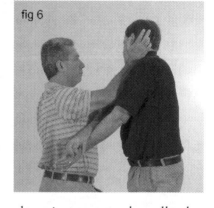

fig 6

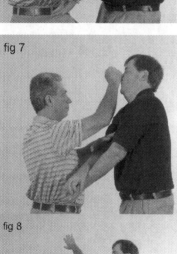

fig 7

neck or jaw area to the collar bone would be a good target. Using the bottom of your fist is called a hammer fist (see fig. 7). This strike can also be used to the nose, face, side of the neck, etc. The list can go on and on, but I think you get the idea.

If you are left handed just replace "right" with "left."

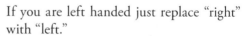

fig 8

What do I do if the opponent is more aggressive and forces me forward? Simple enough—step up to 1:30 with the left foot (see fig. 8) instead of back with the right, and continue the rest of the moves.

Japanese Stranglehold (*rear forearm choke*)

- As the opponent tries to apply the choke, step into a square horse stance toward his open side (the side where the hand is; in this case to the left) (see fig.1). This will open the center line of your opponent and expose several vital targets. As in the photos, work this as if it were a right forearm grab from behind; therefore step with the left and use the right arm for striking.

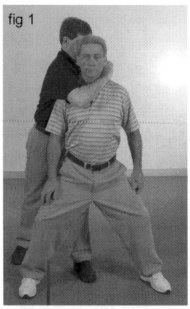

fig 1

- Variation A: Bring your right arm straight out in front and then back as fast as possible, striking the opponent's solar plexus with your elbow (see fig. 2a front view & 2b side view) Note: your left hand is used as a guard throughout the elbow, hammer fist, and

fig 2a

fig 2b

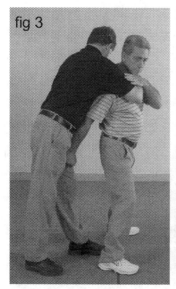

claw/elbow to chin variations or the right hammer fist to groin (see fig. 3, side view of hammer fist). You could combine the elbow and hammer fist. If the situation calls for more drastic action, you can also grab the groin with a right claw and lift your right elbow straight up into the throat and/or chin (see fig. 4, front view of claw and grab & fig. 5, front view of bringing elbow up to the targets). Note: when you strike the solar plexus with the right elbow, you could also strike with the left, using an eye

spear (see fig. 6, side view). Notice the fingers for the eye spear are bent slightly and locked, so as not to jamb or break any fingers. This technique is not usually taught; do not use the eye spear unless you feel your life is in danger, as this may blind the opponent. For eye spear hand formation, see fig. 6 in the next technique, Fang of the Cobra.

Fang of the Cobra (*front two-handed choke*)
There are two ways to do this technique. One can do more damage than the other. Be sure to *read the explanations carefully* so you do not do more damage than necessary.

- Drop your chin to your chest to make it more difficult to be

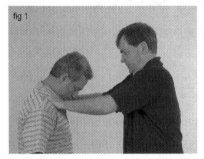

choked (see fig. 1). At the same time step forward with your right foot between the opponent's feet as your left arm traps and pulls down on top of the wrists of the opponent (see fig. 2). Using the right hand with the palm up, keeping the fingers together and slightly bent and locked (see fig. 3), drive fingertips into opponent's throat between opponent's arms (see fig. 4). Note: if you don't need to damage the opponent to this extent, you could use an upward palm strike into the chin (see fig. 5).

- Bring your right hand down, around, and over top and separate, bend, and lock your fingers (see fig. 6); drive fingertips into the opponent's eyes (see fig. 7). Note:

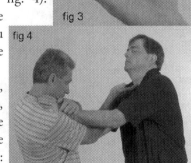

As stated before, you could gear down the strike by thrusting a
palm into the nose of the opponent (see fig. 8). At this point, if

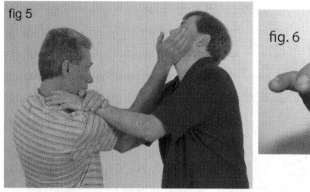

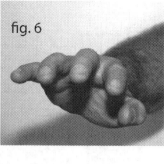

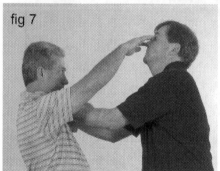

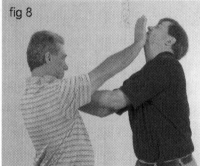

needed, finish with same ending as Knee of Vengeance: grab and
pull into right knee, right forearm, and, if needed, right hammer
fist to groin.

If the opponent stops the attack and tries to get away at any point during this
technique, stop what you are doing—the technique worked.

In the next few techniques we will learn defenses against attempted bear hugs
from the front and rear, with arms pinned and arms free.

Rising Elbow (*bear hug from behind; arms are pinned*)

- Step to the right into a square horse stance, opening up the center line (see fig. 1).
- Strike the opponent's groin with left hammer fist (see fig. 2).

Cat step behind opponent with left foot; i.e., slide your left foot toward the right foot (see fig. 3); when your right foot is clear of the

fig 1

fig 2

fig 3

fig 4

opponent's foot, slide the left foot behind opponent (see fig. 4).
- Drive left claw to groin and grab (see fig. 5).
- While grabbing groin with left claw lift up and drive left elbow up into the chin, drive opponent back over left knee while striking with right hammer fist to groin (see fig. 6).

Circling Elbows (*rear bear hug, arms free*)

- Step into square horse stance with the right foot (see fig. 1).
- If the bear hug is low (see fig. 2), circle your arms around and

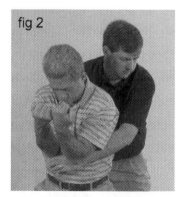

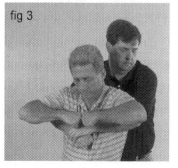

drive your elbows into tops of opponent's hands. If the grab is high, make a fist with both hands and drive your knuckles into tops of hands (see fig. 3).

- As you cat step behind the opponent with your left foot, prepare hands at right hip (see fig. 4).

- Upon planting your right foot behind opponent, strike with your left elbow to the chest or face (do not aim for any specific target) and send a right hammer fist to the groin as you twist your body counterclockwise (see fig. 5), driving the opponent back and over left knee. Note: if you don't break the hold, still cat step behind the opponent and complete the technique, it will still work even if he or she holds on.

Knee Lift (*front bear hug, arms pinned*)

- Stomp on opponent's nearest foot with your right foot (see fig. 1).
- Make two fists and brace your thumbs against index fingers (see fig. 2), then drive thumbs into groin (see fig. 3).

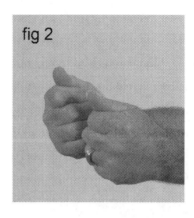

- Lift your right knee to groin (see fig. 4).
- Bring right palm heel up to the chin, face, or chest of the opponent; while striking with right palm, stomp opponent's nearest foot (see fig. 5). Note: the left hand is used as a check to opponent's right arm.

Front Bear Hug (*front bear hug, arms free*)

This technique gives you many different choices. With the first, you can use also on Knee Lift. As the opponent is reaching to grab you, step straight back with your left foot and shoot your left palm to the chin (see fig. 1) at the same time. Then sweep a counterclockwise right reverse hammer fist to the side of the opponent's head (fig. 2). Note: when making a fist, be sure to place your

thumb over the middle finger to avoid jamming your thumb; also keep your elbow slightly bent and locked to avoid hyperextending the elbow. However, if

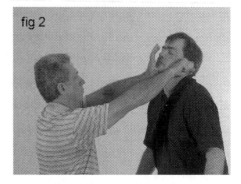

you are grabbed and picked up off the ground, you can box the ears using the palm of both hands (see fig. 3). If it is a serious situation and *your life is in danger*, you could grab the sides of the opponent's head with both hands and drive your thumbs into the eyes (see fig. 4). Please note that driving thumbs into the eyes would probably blind the opponent, so be absolutely sure you need this type of move.

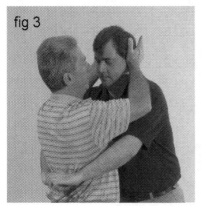

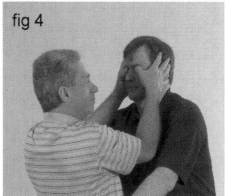

Full Nelson (*full nelson grab*)

After the opponent grabs you and before he pushes you forward and down, you can stop him by grabbing your right wrist with your left hand and placing the left wrist on your forehead and pushing against the aggression. This will keep him from pushing you down. Fig. 1 is a front view of this countermove; fig. 2 is a side view. However, if you are already moving forward and your upper body is bending over, the following is a good technique.

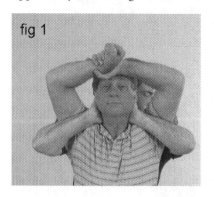
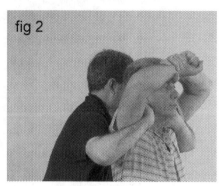

- Step to the right into a square horse stance (see fig. 3).
- Use the force of the opponent pushing you over to strike the groin; with the left hand using a claw, grab the groin (see fig. 4).

- Just as in Rising Elbow, cat step behind the opponent with left foot while left claw is grabbing the groin. Lift your left elbow, striking the chin, and add a right hammer fist to groin at the same time.

Rotating your body counterclockwise drives the opponent over your left knee, taking him down (see fig. 5 & 6).

Everyone has heard the saying "practice makes perfect," but the truth is that "perfect practice makes perfect." The previous nine techniques are a very small sample of what you can do to protect yourself. As stated in the beginning of this chapter, do not attempt to become proficient in these or any other move you learn from a book or video. Get training from an experienced, qualified instructor at a reputable school. Shop around, make phone calls, and observe classes before you get involved with any martial arts school or studio.

Use different objects for defense, such as keys, a cane or even a scarf or belt. Using what is at hand and available when necessary only happens when you change the way you think. Being prepared mentally and ready to act and react is the first step.

Only after you learn how to think in terms of defending yourself and how to use your arms and legs properly would you even attempt to learn how to use a belt, small rope, or scarf to defend yourself. Therefore, I will only cover the use of your keys as a weapon. The term *keys* can refer to any type of projectile, such as an ink pen, pencil, or any other item in your pocket or purse.

When instructed on how to use their keys, most women are told to put them between their fingers. This is usually done during a quick one-hour or one-afternoon course on self-defense. However, I have found the best way to hold the keys is between first knuckle of the thumb and index finger, as if you were going to use the key to open a door (see fig. 1). This gives you more penetration and a stronger grip than if you place them between your fingers (see fig. 2).

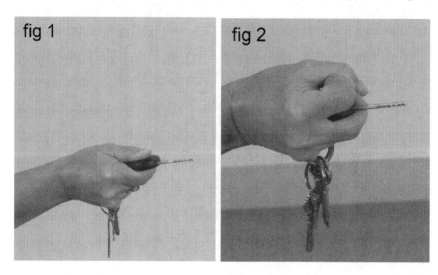

When placed between the fingers, if you try to swipe across the face or use it in a slashing motion, you take the chance of damaging the web between your fingers. If you are grabbed and your arms and hands are free to move, use the key as a jabbing instrument. Keep jabbing at different targets and in different directions until the opponent retreats. *Do not strike just once and hope that the assailant will back off and leave you alone.* To help you practice these strikes, have your helper dress in old clothing and use a marker as the striking instrument. Be careful of the power you use, as a marker can still hurt. Speed and accuracy are important with this type of defense. Also, remember to use knees, elbows, and anything else from some of the previous techniques along with the key. The next several photos are some of the grabs and targets that may be used.

Study the next twelve photos for using the key to stab or jab the targeted areas.

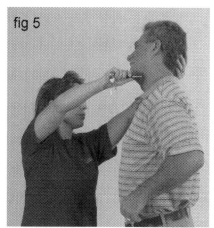

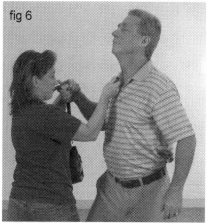

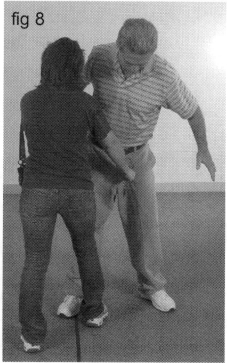

fig 9

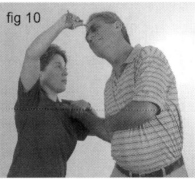

fig 10

fig 11

fig 12

The author is available for seminars for all types of groups and businesses. Send requests for seminars to the address below. A video is available that will demonstrate the techniques in chapter 7. At the end of the video is a brief demonstration about how to use items, such as a key, pen, cane, belt, scarf, and many other everyday items, as self-defense weapons. Just pay $9.95 for shipping and handling of the video. This fee applies to the forty-eight states in the continental United States. Addresses outside of the continental United Stated should include extra postage for shipping. Send cashier's check or money order only; no personal checks or credit cards will be accepted. Please do not send cash. Just send proof of purchase (store receipt or receipt from internet payment), payment (cashier's check or money order payable to Aware & Prepared Video Offer C/O Ronald K. Hanzel), and your correct name and mailing address to:

Aware and Prepared Video Offer
P.O. Box 33646
N. Royalton, Ohio 44133